To Brittany S.
from Mick Fynn
5-22-99
Congradulations
Best Wishe
Always!

Learning by Heart

Contemporary

Learning

American Poetry

by Heart

about School

EDITED BY

Maggie Anderson &

David Hassler

FOREWORD BY

ROBERT COLES

University of Iowa Press

University of Iowa Press,
Iowa City 52242
Copyright © 1999 by the
University of Iowa Press
All rights reserved
Printed in the United States of America
Design by Richard Hendel
http://www.uiowa.edu/~uipress
Printed on acid-free paper
Library of Congress
Cataloging-in-Publication Data
Learning by heart: contemporary American poetry
about school / edited by Maggie Anderson and
David Hassler; foreword by Robert Coles.
     p.   cm.
   ISBN 0-87745-662-3, ISBN 0-87745-663-1 (pbk.)
   1. American poetry—20th century.
2. Education—Poetry. 3. Schools—Poetry.
I. Anderson, Maggie. II. Hassler, David,
1964— .
PS595.E38L4 1999
811'.54080355—dc21   98-47405

99 00 01 02 03 C 5 4 3 2 1
99 00 01 02 03 P 5 4 3 2 1

TO OUR TEACHERS

AND OUR STUDENTS

And you America,

Cast you the real reckoning for your present?

The lights and shadows of your future, good or evil?

To girlhood, boyhood look, the teacher and the school.

—Walt Whitman

from "An Old Man's Thought of School"

Contents

4. RECESS

Foreword

ROBERT COLES

. . . . . .

The poet and physician William Carlos Williams was for many years a school doctor in New Jersey. He'd examine children "on the premises," he once said, and thereafter dispatch them home or tell them they were well enough to remain in the classroom. He kept a record of sorts from day to day as he went about doing his medical work, because he was quite taken by what he called "the daily drama" of all the children coming and going, growing and learning. "There's a poem a minute taking place in those classrooms," he once told an admiring medical student who was asking him about his clinical life, where it was practiced, and with whom. As I went through the poems that make up this book I thought of Dr. Williams's remark, but I thought also of the broad range of his writing. He was a close observer of his neighbors and fellow citizens, and he always tried hard to respond in verse (and in the fiction he also wrote) to what his eyes noticed and his ears heard. True, like all poets, he called on his inner world and used images and figures of speech to convey what his mind had imagined, what it wanted to suggest. But he insisted on connecting his talent with words to observable instances, to the incidents and rhythms of a particular life, spent in a particular place. Hence the important opening lines in the second book of *Paterson*: "Outside / outside myself / there is a world, / he rumbled, subject to my incursions / —a world / (to me) at rest, / Which I approach / concretely—."

Here then are "incursions" rendered in verse—dozens of poems meant to make the reader remember going to elementary school and high school or meant to give the reader pause, to prompt some reflection on what happens in those classrooms, on the way to and from them or outside them, on the playing fields or the streets. Most of our ideas about what is called education are supplied to us by social scientists of one kind or another. As a result, theory rules the day in schools where men and women learn to be teachers— book after book filled with generalizations, formulations, paradigms. I know what happens as a consequence, because for years I have taught a seminar attended by young teachers, and they let me know all the sociological and psychological ideas that have filled their heads. But I want another angle of approach for them, and so we read fiction that evokes school life in one way or another—stories by Tobias Wolff and Richard Yates and Charles Baxter, lyrical nonfiction by James Agee, and novels by Hardy, Dickens, Salinger, Silone, and Toni Morrison, in which teachers and students figure, or children who clearly have gone awry, as happens among some boys and girls in any school district. At first my students have trouble making what they often call "the connection" between what they have read and what they have learned (in all their many theory-bound courses) to regard as worthy of attention. Only gradually do they begin to realize what is being given to them—but also what is being asked of them: stories that evoke the complexity of things, that tell of ironies and paradoxes and inconsistencies and contradictions, in contrast indeed with the endlessly reductionist learning so often offered in the name of "educational psychology" or "sociology."

Now, the same young teachers and, one hopes and prays, thousands of others across the land, will have a chance to think about schooling, as Dr. Williams suggested, "concretely," through the evocations (and provocations) of talented poets, who want to tell of moments, of instances, of things done or left undone, of "times when," as my fifth-grade teacher, Bernicia Avery, would put it. She would announce a "times when" period, in which we were invited, any of us, to stand up and tell a story about something that had happened to us. We loved those occasions, because we were free at last of rote memorization, of unquestioning compliance with rules and mandates and arbitrary customs (as in spelling!) of various kinds. Rather, we were allowed—better, encouraged—to let our minds find their own direction, have their own say in their own way. I can still remember, in that regard, a classmate, nine-year-old Sally Davis, reading to us a poem she wrote one "time when": she'd tried to "catch" a robin, and the robin, apparently, didn't simply fly away, but hopped, skipped, jumped, or as she put it, "short-flied" across her lawn, by which she meant to convey the brief spurts of elevation summoned by a playful (or was it hungry?) bird, distracted from a feeder by a girl who wanted to draw dangerously near. The poem was put in the form of an address from Sally to this "robin red-breast." The poem asked why—why the distrust, when no harm was meant, rather a gesture of friendliness. "But nature said no"—and here I am, a half-century later, remembering those four words, the simple, direct beauty of them, their various implications.

So, too, memory will be energized for those who read these poems—teachers and their students, any of us. We all have experienced what these poets have wanted to relate, embody in words. We all have been "beginners," have struggled with "spelling" and with "penmanship," have known afterward the "nostalgia" that goes with remembering a school building, have yearned for (or feared) "recess," have taken rides on "school buses," have heard the teacher say, "the thing you must remember," have gone to our "first practice," have waited and waited for that time called "lunch," have known "cruel boys" and "sunny days" and a "bully" and seen "cheerleaders" and listened to "the high school band" and gone to "the junior high dance" and later on (as with me just now) experienced "gratitude to old teachers"—and these are just a few of the matters addressed in the poems whose titles I have worked into this sentence (which clearly could have gone on and on). What follows, then, is a wonderfully lively and compelling collection, a unique one indeed, and one that will wake us all up, provoke feeling and thought aplenty, stir and jar minds, prompt all of us, who every day can teach and learn from one another, to stop and look inward, recall through the words of others what it means to be human, to have a mind that engages knowingly with others, with this world—the heart of what school does for children, as Williams's verse reminds us.

Editors' Note

The idea for *Learning by Heart: Contemporary American Poetry about School* evolved through our own experiences as poets-in-the-schools and our conversations with elementary and secondary teachers throughout the country. Time and again, we met teachers who were compiling their own collections of contemporary poems about school. Some teachers used these packets to encourage their students to write poems and others used them to instruct future teachers in teacher-training workshops. We had our own folders of poems that we used in poetry classes with children and adults, as well as in teacher writing workshops. Thus, the work of this anthology began years ago, unselfconsciously, in some ways spontaneously, among teachers and poets who share a passion for poetry.

We considered over 700 contemporary American poems and chose 135 poems in a variety of styles and tones from over 100 poets. Although many poets have written well about college and university experiences, we chose only poems about primary and secondary school. We selected no more than two poems by any one poet. The earliest publication date for any poem in this anthology is 1947. Although some poems written in the 1940s or 1950s look back to earlier decades, we chose what we think are the best and most broadly representative poems about the school experience over the last fifty years. Of the poets assembled here, many are well known and widely published; some are less well known, emerging writers; and a few have never published before. All the poets have been students, and many have taught in a primary or secondary school. Interestingly, more than 90 percent of these writers have worked at one time or another as poets-in-the-schools. We arranged these poems thematically to suggest their connections and to create a conversation among them.

The poems in *Learning by Heart* remember, celebrate, and censure. In reading them, we are reminded how our lives are shaped by our school experiences and the stubborn persistence of our memories. Everyone has a school story: of a teacher or a coach; of a time when we knew all the answers, or the time when we didn't;

of our earliest friends and enemies and their unforgettable names. As Walt Whitman wrote in 1874 for the inauguration of a public school in Camden, New Jersey:

> Only a lot of boys and girls?
> Only the tiresome spelling, writing, ciphering classes?
> Only a public school?
>
> Ah more, infinitely more . . .

We are grateful to the following people who helped us in our search for poems about school and who helped us locate some of the poets: Robert Bly, Chris Cotton, Bob Fox, Maurice Kilwein Guevara, Marc Harshman, Donald M. Hassler, Terry Hermsen, Julia Kasdorf, Philip Levine, Gina Mackintosh, Irene McKinney, Naomi Shihab Nye, Sheila Ritzmann, John and Lynn Sollers, William Studebaker, James and Pauline Thornton, and Paul Zimmer.

We also thank the Ohio Arts Council for a 1997 poetry fellowship and Kent State University for a 1997–1998 professional improvement leave for Maggie Anderson; the Ohio Arts Council for David Hassler's poet-in-the-school residencies during 1997–1998; the Wick Poetry Program and the Department of English at Kent State University; and Ted and Michael Lyons for manuscript preparation. Finally, we are grateful to Anna French and Lynn Gregor, who have made this project a part of their lives too.

1 / Homeroom

Painting the North San Juan School

GARY SNYDER

. . . . . .

White paint splotches on blue head bandanas
Dusty transistor with wired-on antenna
    plays sixties rock and roll;
Little kids came with us are on teeter-totters
    tilting under shade of oak
This building good for ten years more.
The shingled bell-cupola trembles
    at every log truck rolling by —

The radio speaks:
    today it will be one hundred degrees in the valley.
— Franquette walnuts grafted on the
    local native rootstock do o.k.
    nursery stock of cherry all has fungus;
Lucky if a bare-root planting lives,

This paint thins with water.
This year the buses will run only
    on paved roads,
Somehow the children will be taught:
How to record their mother tongue
    with written signs,

Names to call the landscape of the continent
                they live on
Assigned it by the ruling people of the last
    three hundred years,
The games of numbers,
What went before, as told by those who
    think they know it,

A drunken man with chestnut mustache
Stumbles off the road to ask if he can help.

Children drinking chocolate milk.

Ladders resting on the shaky porch.

The School Children

LOUISE GLÜCK

. . . . . .

The children go forward with their little satchels.
And all morning the mothers have labored
to gather the late apples, red and gold,
like words of another language.

And on the other shore
are those who wait behind great desks
to receive these offerings.

How orderly they are — the nails
on which the children hang
their overcoats of blue or yellow wool.

And the teachers shall instruct them in silence
and the mothers shall scour the orchards
    for a way out,
drawing to themselves the gray limbs of the fruit trees
bearing so little ammunition.

Taking My Son to School

EAMON GRENNAN

. . . . . .

His first day. Waiting, he plays
By himself in the garden.
I take a photo he clowns for,
Catching him, as it were, in flight.

All the way there in the car he chatters
And sings, giving me directions.
There are no maps for this journey:
It is the wilderness we enter.

Around their tall bespectacled teacher,
A gaggle of young ones in summer colours.
Silent, he stands on their border,
Clutching a bunch of purple dahlias.

Shyly he offers them up to her.
Distracted she holds them upside down.
He teeters on the rim of the circle,
Head drooping, a flower after rain.

I kiss him goodbye and leave him:
Stiff, he won't meet my eye.
I drive by him but he doesn't wave.
In my mind I rush to his rescue.

The distance bleeding between us,
I steal a last look back:
From a thicket of blondes, brunettes,
His red hair blazes.

It is done. I have handed him over.
I remember him wildly dancing
Naked and shining, shining
In the empty garden.

Schoolboys with Dog, Winter

WILLIAM MATTHEWS

. . . . . .

It's dark when they scuff off to school.
It's good to trample the thin panes of casual
ice along the track where twice a week

a freight that used to stop here lugs grain
and radiator hoses past us to a larger town.
It's good to cloud the paling mirror

of the dawn sky with your mouthwashed breath,
and to thrash and stamp against the way
you've been overdressed and pudged

into your down jacket like a pastel
sausage, and to be cruel to the cringing
dog and then to thump it and hug it and croon

to it nicknames. At last the pale sun rolls
over the horizon. And look!
The frosted windows of the schoolhouse gleam.

Spring Glen Grammar School

D O N A L D   H A L L

. . . . . .

THAT

I remember the moment because I planned, at six in the first grade,
to remember the moment forever. For weeks we memorized the
        alphabet,
reciting it in unison singsong, copying it in block capitals
on paper with wide lines, responding to letters on flashcards —
but we learned no words.
                        Then we heard: "Tomorrow we start to read."
Miss Stephanie Ford wrote on the blackboard, in huge letters,
T H A T. "That," she said, pointing her wooden stick, "is 'that.'"

POLITICS

Each year began in September with a new room and a new teacher:
I started with Stephanie Ford, then Miss Flint, Miss Sudell
whom I loved, Miss Stroker, Miss Fehm, Miss Pikosky . . .
                                            At assemblies
I was announcer. I was elected Class President in the eighth grade,
not because they liked me — it wasn't a popularity contest —
but because I was polite to grown-ups, spoke distinctly,
kept my shirt tucked in, and combed my hair: I was presidential.

THE BOX

Eight years of Spring Glen Grammar School. If I should live
to be eighty, this box would contain the tithe of everything.
In the glass case there's a rock garden with tiny snails, mosses,
infinitesimal houses, sidewalks, scissors and crayons, teachers,
and a model of Spring Glen Grammar School.
                                    See, the doors swing
open; see, small pupils gather around a boy in blue knickers.
The box is humid; it continues to continue: Nothing escapes.

Teacher

AUDRE LORDE

. . . . . .

I make my children promises in wintry afternoons
like lunchtime stories
when my feet hurt from talking too much
and not enough movement except in my own
worn down at the heel shoes
except in the little circle of broken down light
I am trapped in
the intensities of my own (our) situation
where what we need and do not have
deadens us
and promises sound like destruction
white snowflakes clog the passages
drifting through the halls and corridors
while I tell stories with no ending
at lunchtime
the children's faces bear uneasy smiles
like a heavy question
I provide food with a frightening efficiency
the talk is free / dom meaning state
condition of being
We are elementary forces colliding in free fall.

And who will say I made promises
better kept in confusion
than time
grown tall and straight in a season of snow
in a harsh time of the sun that withers
who will say as they build
ice castles at noon
living the promises I made
these children
who will say
look—we have laid out new cities
with more love than our dreams

Who will hear
freedom's bell deaden
in the clang of the gates of the prisons
where snow-men melt into darkness
unforgiven and so remembered
while the hot noon speaks in a fiery voice?

How we romped through so many winters
made snowballs play at war
rubbing snow against our brown faces
and they tingled and grew bright
in the winter sun
instead of chocolate we rolled snow
over our tongues
until it melted like sugar
burning the cracks in our lips
and we shook our numbed fingers
all the way home
remembering
summer was coming.

As the promises I make children
sprout like wheat from early spring's wager
who will hear freedom
ring in the chains of promise
who will forget the curse
of the outsider
who will not recognize our season
as free
who will say
Promise corrupts
what it does not invent.

Home

MARILYN NELSON

. . . . . .

I neither remember
the first time
nor the last.

Only once
another child
in a pink dress
stood on her father's lawn
barefooted,
her eyes hard with laughter
as I walked by.

I remember
a first day at school.
Someone met me on the playground,
smiled with me
past teeter-totters
bobbing like oil derricks
and the slide shining gold
in the sun.
That time
a sixth-grader
looked our way,
aimed his eyes carefully,
and shot me with
america.

Cruel Boys

GARY SOTO

. . . . . .

First day. Jackie and I walking in leaves
On our way to becoming 8th graders,
Pencils behind our ears, pee-chee folders
Already scribbled with football players
In dresses, track star in a drooped bra.
We're tough. I'm Mexican
And he's an unkillable Okie with three
Teeth in his pocket, sludge under
His nails from scratching oily pants.
No one's going to break us, not the dean
Or principal, not the cops
Who could arrive in pairs, walkie-talkies
To their mouths, warning:

"Dangerous. They have footballs."
We could bounce them off their heads
And reporters might show up
With shirt sleeves rolled up to their ears,
Asking our age, if we're Catholic.
But this never happens. We go to first
Period, math, then second period, geography,
And in third period, English, the woman
Teacher reads us Frost, something
About a tree, and to set things straight,
How each day will fall like a tree.
Jackie raises his hand, stands up,
And shouts, "You ain't nothing but a hound dog,"
As the spitballs begin to fly.

Beginners

M A R K   D O T Y

. . . . . .

The year Miss Tynes enrolled our class
in the Object of the Month Club,
a heavy box arrived each month
from the Metropolitan Museum.
What emerged once—when volunteers
opened each latch, and one lucky girl

lifted the wooden lid away—
was an Egyptian cat, upright on its haunches,
unapproachable, one golden earring flashing,
a carved cartouche between its legs.
Miss Tynes read a translation of the hieroglyphics
and a paragraph depicting the glory

of thousands of mummies ranged on shelves
in the dark—cased and muslined cats,
ibis, baboons—their jewelry ready to offer
any sliver of sunlight back, if it ever touched them.
Later, the cat ruled the back of the room,
fixed on a countertop beside a model

of the planets and a display of moths.
When we'd finished our work it was all right
to go and stand beside it,
even, if we were careful, touch it.
I'd read a story in which two children
drank an emerald medicine from a pharmacy urn

forgot their parents, and understood
the speech of cats. Their adventures were nocturnal
and heroic, and their cat became, I think,
the King of Cats, and was lost to them,
so they drank red medicine from the drugstore urn,
and returned to the human world

of speech. I cried, not for their lost pet
but for the loss of language, and my father
forbade me sad books. Some days, after school,
I'd go to my friend Walter's, and we'd play
a simple game: because he was smaller than me,
though no younger, Walter would be the son.

He'd take off his shirt and sit in my lap;
I'd put my arms around him
and rub his stomach, and he would pretend
to cry or be content, liking my hands.
We were ten, or eight. It's too easy
to think of our game as sex before we knew

what bodies could do, before bodies could do
much. There was something else,
at least for me: the pleasure
of touching what became pure form,
not Walter anymore but the sensation
of skin over supple muscle. I was the heroic

father, I loved—not him, exactly,
with his narrow crewcut head which reminded me,
even then, of a mouse—but the formal thing
he'd become in his room, with the door closed.
We never changed roles; I was the good lover,
I fathered him. We knew enough to keep

the game private, less out of guilt
than a sense of something exposure
might dilute. It was like the way the children
in my class touched the cat, even talked to it,
hesitantly, beginners in a new language,
maybe imagined it might speak back to us.

Though it was the perfect confidant,
since it could take in anything

and remain calm and black and golden
until it was packed away in the varnished box
to another school, where other children
might lean toward it and whisper,
until it was more ancient, with all it knew.

Our Room

MOLLY PEACOCK

. . . . . .

I tell the children in school sometimes
why I hate alcoholics: my father was one.
"Alcohol" and "disease" I use, and shun
the word "drunk" or even "drinking," since one time
the kids burst out laughing when I told them.
I felt as though they were laughing at me.
I waited for them, wounded, remem-
bering how I imagined they'd howl at me
when I was in grade 5. Acting drunk
is a guaranteed screamer, especially
for boys. I'm quiet when I sort the junk
of my childhood for them, quiet so we
will all be quiet, and they can ask what
questions they have to and tell about what
happened to them, too. The classroom becomes
oddly lonely when we talk about our homes.

Sunny Days

MOLLY PEACOCK

. . . . . .

The children are singing a song about
morning where they all put their arms over
their heads to show the sun coming out,
then turn in their places, dip, then uncover
their arms to show the sun again. They are
all concentrating hard, the grown-up-acting
Spanish girls, the babyish blonder girls far-
ther into the room. All this is taxing
after numbering and reading and drawing
and praying and eating just right and sharing,
the polyester habit gently whirring
out from the hips of Sister Roseann. Carrying
the burden of always being sunny
is too hard. Yet the kids try for sunny:
begonias, Sister Roseann, recess, milk,
the weedy sidewalk, watching a pimp bilk
one of his girls on 6th Street and hearing
her shriek, watching one of the girls ignoring
Roseann, who grabs her, and hearing her shriek.
The meek scream and the masters are meek
as they bring mistakes to light. The girls take
darkness and put it behind their eyes. They make
homes for themselves behind their screams and lies.

The Sandhills, Early Winter

HILDA RAZ

. . . . .

The girl in the back row sits perfectly still,
doesn't answer my unspoken question
about her pajama top, why she wears it
as a blouse today in school, fifth period
when I teach her class, or why her eye
is bruised shut, her glasses broken
in the same lens, her skin cut.

Or why her paper is tattooed with hearts
and arrows, broken in places under the ink,
for yesterday's lesson,
and today's is blank and she's slumped

when I bend over to brush the page
with my palm and ask questions
the other kids hear, about sounds and smells,
the texture of wind on gravel, on hard ice.

But as I move on, she bends to write
what I'd rather not read
in the gym corner office behind the stage
and later I wave in the face of the principal.
I read her lines out loud and when I'm finished,
he says a sentence coupling nouns and verbs
in a way I've never heard before
and ends by saying, "No,
No, we've tried, we can't do anything."

That night I buy her a bus ticket
out of there, drive fifty miles to the Greyhound
station and click her seatbelt shut before the motor starts

and again, a plane ticket for where it's warm
and the close sun heals
and take her home to my daughter's room

I drive to her trailer house in the country and when
her uncles and father come to the door,
her brothers behind them, I smile and say
I'm the visiting teacher and we've got a problem

and on Friday, as always, I'm out of there.

Room 19, Eakin Elementary

DIANE GILLIAM FISHER

.　.　.　.　.　.

There's a boys' line and a girls' line
in Miss Sharp's room, and line leaders.
Three reading groups—Lions, Tigers, and Zebras.

Miss Sharp tells you once,
then it's up to you. Remember what you are.
It's not allowed visiting with your neighbor.

It's not allowed poking your pencil
through your milk carton for the straw,
you get lead poisoning.

It's not allowed telling what you dreamed
for sharing, you have to bring something
people can see. You have to write

with fat pencils that make you
write slower. When you write capital letters,
go almost to the top line, but don't

touch it, it's poison. When it's free time,
you have to use it wisely. When it's recess,
girls hold hands and march

between the tetherballs, teachers, and boys,
and sing with their faces
pushed out real far—

We don't stop for nobody
We don't stop for nobody

Zimmer's Head Thudding against the Blackboard

PAUL ZIMMER

. . . . . .

At the blackboard I had missed
Five number problems in a row,
And was about to foul a sixth,
When the old exasperated nun
Began to pound my head against
My six mistakes. When I cried,
She threw me back into my seat,
Where I hid my head and swore
That very day I'd be a poet,
And curse her yellow teeth with this.

Two-Room Schoolhouse

NANCE VAN WINCKEL

. . . . .

Mt. Vernon, Virginia, 1958

When I'm bad I'm given ten white pages.
If I make my letters tall, I can make them
toe the lines. I can plant a row of t's,
then another, crossing and recrossing
every black stunted stem along the way.

Often we work alone like this, grades 1–3.
From the loft upstairs, our teacher's a dream
who climbs down to us. The devil's wind
bangs on the window, and she steps down.
Say I don't remember something right,
I get to sit quiet at my desk until I do.

Then I think of the big door up the road,
the bad wind banging there too, long ago.
And the old father in his wooden teeth
getting up to answer. I watch him disappear,
though the teeth remain—two rows
of splinters on a glass shelf.

Teacher's slow on the rungs, pausing
to remind us that anyone who works hard
can plant himself deep into history, send out
taproots of dull intervening incidents.
We say the lesson back, and back again,
until the white wig falls off
and we forget our good manners—
our laughter too loud at the school play.

And who's laughing loudest, whose little teeth
clattering towards a table edge,
then winding down to just that smile
without its face? I've been trying
to remember this right, the wrong I did,
having sat here quietly all morning.

Hotel Nights with My Mother

LINDA McCARRISTON

. . . . . .

The hometown flophouse
was what she could afford
the nights he came after us
with a knife. I'd grab my books,
already dreading the next day's
explanations of homework undone
—*I ran out of paper*—the lies
I'd invent standing in front of
the nuns in the clothes I'd lain in
full-bladdered all night, a flimsy
chair-braced door between us
and the hallway's impersonal riot.

Years later, then, in the next
city, standing before my first class,
I scanned the rows of faces,
their cumulative skill in the
brilliant adolescent dances
of self-presentation, of hiding.
New teacher, looking young, seeming
gullible, I know, I let them
give me any excuse and took it.
I was watching them all

for the dark-circled eyes,
yesterday's crumpled costume, the marks
—the sorrowful coloring of marks—
the cuticles flaming and torn.
I made of myself each day a chink
a few might pass through unscathed.

The Sacred

STEPHEN DUNN

. . . . . .

After the teacher asked if anyone had
   a sacred place
and the students fidgeted and shrunk

in their chairs, the most serious of them all
   said it was his car,
being in it alone, his tape deck playing

things he'd chosen, and others knew the truth
   had been spoken
and began speaking about their rooms,

their hiding places, but the car kept coming
   up, the car in motion,
music filling it, and sometimes one other person

who understood the bright altar of the dashboard
   and how far away
a car could take him from the need

to speak, or to answer, the key
   in having a key
and putting it in, and going.

Poet in Residence at a Country School

DON WELCH

. . . . . .

The school greets me like a series
of sentence fragments sent out to recess.
Before I hit the front door
I'm into a game of baseball soccer.
My first kick's a foul; my second sails
over the heads of the outfielders;
rounding third base, I suck in my stomach
and dodge the throw of a small blue-eyed boy.
I enter the school, sucking apples of wind.
In the fifth-grade section of the room
I stand in the corner of an old rug and ask,
Where would you go where no one could find you,
a secret place where you'd be invisible
to everyone except yourselves?
What would you do there; what would you say?
I ask them to imagine they're there,
and writing a poem. As I walk around the room,
I look at the wrists of the kids,
green and alive, careful with silence.
They are writing themselves into fallen elms,
corners of barns, washouts, and alkali flats.
I watch until a tiny boy approaches,
who says he can't think of a place,
who wonders today, at least,
if he just couldn't sit on my lap.
Tomorrow, he says, he'll write.
And so the two of us sit under a clock,
beside a gaudy picture of a butterfly,
and a sweet poem of Christina Rosetti's.
And in all that silence, neither of us
can imagine where he'd rather be.

Letter to a Substitute Teacher

GARY GILDNER

· · · · ·

Dear Miss Miller,
You are someone
too sweet to sleep alone
and I can't help myself

sitting here hearing
your soft voice so
I must tell you
I like you

very much and would like
to know you better.
I know there is a difference
in our age and race

but we do have something
in common—You're a girl
and I'm a boy
and that is all

we need. Please
do not look at me
like I'm silly or sick
and most of all

please do not reject
my very first love
affair. If you do
not feel the same

as I do please
tell me how I can forget
your unforgettable voice
that reminds me

of Larry the Duke's pet
birds in the morning,
your blue eyes like the
Blessed Virgin's,

your golden hair and your
nice red mouth. Please
give me some sign
of how you feel,

I would rather be hurt
than forgotten forever.
Sincerely yours,
The Boy in the Green Shirt.

Waiting

PEG MCNALLY

. . . . . .

I am the lowest paid substitute teacher in the district.
Everyday, five days a week, I drive my father's used car towards
the big lake to the northeast corner of Hough and 79th, at which
point I turn right, easing the four-door Mercury Cougar, mud
flaps and all, down the ramp into the first available space in the
underground garage of Addison Junior High School, where I'll
teach five classes back to back without so much as a coffee break
and all of this depressing me no end on this particular morning,
until I think about my date last night, and in this minute of
memory, I believe this dating just might lead to bigger things,
maybe even marriage, and this concept of spending the rest of
my life in wedded bliss allows my pace to quicken, allows me to
pass the other teachers in the hall without so much as a "Hello,"
which doesn't bother me at all, because after all, I'm only a sub, a
bench-warmer, a stand-in, someone who's required to check-in
to the main office every day to pick up my assignments and class
lists which have the names of all the students I'll never really
know as well as I have come to know the daily specials in the
cafeteria, and it is this thought that moves me right past the
office to the teachers' lounge, where I hope someone has brought
in those sugar doughnuts that I really have come to love so
much, love more than the idea of teaching seventh graders the
meaning of a poem, the rhythm of language, because after all,
I'm just a sub who'll finish her day at three, head far enough
south to reach her father's house, where, at dinner, he'll ask how
my day went, and I'll say, "Fine," and he'll remind me that this
job might lead to a full-time position, something permanent,
maybe with benefits, but I really don't want that, because I've
seen what teaching school is like, and the phone rings, and it's
my date from last night, and he asks if I'm busy this weekend,
and I told him I promised my father I'd do some things around

the house, and promises to my father have become sacred since my mother died, so I might even wash the car, it's the least I can do now that he lets me drive it everyday, five days a week towards the big lake, to the northeast corner of Hough and 79th, and you know the rest.

Gee, You're So Beautiful
That It's Starting to Rain

RICHARD BRAUTIGAN

· · · · · ·

Oh, Marcia,
I want your long blonde beauty
to be taught in high school,
so kids will learn that God
lives like music in the skin
and sounds like a sunshine harpsicord.
I want high school report cards
   to look like this:

Playing with Gentle Glass Things
   A

Computer Magic
   A

Writing Letters to Those You Love
   A

Finding out about Fish
   A

Marcia's Long Blonde Beauty
   A+!

The Teacher Said

DARA WIER

. . . . . .

Imagine someone you love is dead.
Now build them the heaven you'd put them in.
Look for heaven in *Life* and *Look* and look
while you're at it for hell. For hell
is another place we'll have to build.
Find a terrible fire, hook and ladders,
red as waxed apples and dark as rich soil.
Look at the ten tiny firemen, already burnt
in their clumsy helmets and coats, someone,
someone's little sister, falling, falling
faster over the safety bars of a seven-story
landing, falling into a safety net on fire.
And find a face so forlorn as it looks on
and feels she's gone. Remember nobody's
heroic, nobody is saved, no one gets out alive.
Paste it to your posters and we'll tack it
to the board. Right next to the ⬥▬
U-T-FULL birds and composite flowers
you drew for your fathers and mothers.
Let's strive to keep our edges just inside
the lines. Remember to ask permission
before cutting out the picture of the corpse
preserved four thousand years in peat.
See how it shines as if a well-paid servant
lovingly rubbed it daily. Take care
when you use your scissors not to run
or climb on rickety chairs. Be obedient,
be tidy, be so careful, be very sweet.

Raising Their Hands

JULIA LISELLA

. . . . . .

Sometimes I dream about my students,
the pink of their palms
red and raw.
One student, seven feet tall,
his long back
hunched over the desk,
his arm out and above him —
he could be waving
or stopping a train.
Another student wears eyeliner for the stage.
She bends from the ribs,
her body forming a tiny "c,"
her hand up sudden as a whitecap.

Some days they frighten me.
Put your hands down, I tell them.
Shout. Explode. Scream it.
Instead they look at me and smile
the way they would at foreigners who don't speak the language.
That's how they've trained me.
Now I wait until I see a scatter of fingers
and then I choose —
Yes, your palm, your hand,
your arched spine,
you with your idea,
Speak.

School Buses

FRANK KOOISTRA

. . . . . .

Six of them: great orange, great golden carp
Lined up at the railroad crossing, red stop fins fanning.
Each waits, each listens, and crosses in turn
Headed for the lily shoals of children.

2 / Language Lessons

Diction

HILDA RAZ

. . . . . .

"God is in the details,"
I tell the kids
in the public school
in Milligan, Nebraska.
They wonder what I mean.
I tell them to look
out the window
at the spring fields
the mud coming up
just to the knee
of the small pig
in the far pasture.
They tell me
it's not a knee
but a hock
and I hadn't ought
to say things I know
nothing about. I say
the light on the mud
is pure chalcedony.
They say the mud
killed two cows
over the weekend.
I tell them the pig
is alive and the spring
trees are standing in a green haze.
They tell me school is out
in a week and they have to plant.
The grain elevator at the end
of Main Street stretches out
her blue arms. The kids say chutes.

Learning in the First Grade

JANE KENYON

. . . . . .

"The cup is red. The drop of rain
is blue. The clam is brown."

So said the sheet of exercises —
purple mimeos, still heady
from the fluid in the rolling
silver drum. But the cup was

not red. It was white,
or had no color of its own.

Oh, but my mind was finical.
It put the teacher perpetually
in the wrong. Called on, however,
I said aloud: "The cup is red."

"But it's not," I thought,
like Galileo Galilei
muttering under his beard . . .

Persimmons

LI-YOUNG LEE

. . . . .

In sixth grade Mrs. Walker
slapped the back of my head
and made me stand in the corner
for not knowing the difference
between *persimmon* and *precision*.
How to choose

persimmons. This is precision.
Ripe ones are soft and brown-spotted.
Sniff the bottoms. The sweet one
will be fragrant. How to eat:
put the knife away, lay down newspaper.
Peel the skin tenderly, not to tear the meat.
Chew the skin, suck it,
and swallow. Now, eat
the meat of the fruit,
so sweet,
all of it, to the heart.

Donna undresses, her stomach is white.
In the yard, dewy and shivering
with crickets, we lie naked,
face-up, face-down.
I teach her Chinese.
Crickets: *chiu chiu*. Dew: I've forgotten.
Naked: I've forgotten.
Ni, wo: you and me.
I part her legs,
remember to tell her
she is beautiful as the moon.

Other words
that got me into trouble were
fight and *fright*, *wren* and *yarn*.

Fight was what I did when I was frightened,
fright was what I felt when I was fighting.
Wrens are small, plain birds,
yarn is what one knits with.
Wrens are soft as yarn.
My mother made birds out of yarn.
I loved to watch her tie the stuff;
a bird, a rabbit, a wee man.

Mrs. Walker brought a persimmon to class
and cut it up
so everyone could taste
a *Chinese apple*. Knowing
it wasn't ripe or sweet, I didn't eat
but watched the other faces.

My mother said every persimmon has a sun
inside, something golden, glowing,
warm as my face.

Once, in the cellar, I found two wrapped in newspaper,
forgotten and not yet ripe.
I took them and set both on my bedroom windowsill,
where each morning a cardinal
sang, *The sun, the sun.*

Finally understanding
he was going blind,
my father sat up all one night
waiting for a song, a ghost.
I gave him the persimmons,
swelled, heavy as sadness,
and sweet as love.

This year, in the muddy lighting
of my parents' cellar, I rummage, looking
for something I lost.
My father sits on the tired, wooden stairs,
black cane between his knees,

hand over hand, gripping the handle.
He's so happy that I've come home.
I ask how his eyes are, a stupid question.
All gone, he answers.

Under some blankets, I find a box.
Inside the box I find three scrolls.
I sit beside him and untie
three paintings by my father:
Hibiscus leaf and a white flower.
Two cats preening.
Two persimmons, so full they want to drop from the cloth.

He raises both hands to touch the cloth,
asks, *Which is this?*

This is persimmons, Father.

Oh, the feel of the wolftail on the silk,
the strength, the tense
precision in the wrist.
I painted them hundreds of times
eyes closed. These I painted blind.
Some things never leave a person:
scent of the hair of one you love,
the texture of persimmons,
in your palm, the ripe weight.

Spanish Lessons

RANE ARROYO

. . . . . .

Today's word: *agua.*
Water, like in your mother's womb.
Water, like in the river
through Jayuya, Puerto Rico.
Water insists there be *thirst*
in the world in order to
be the source of songs.

Yesterday's word: *amarillo.*

The word in Spanish
has the "y" sound as
in yellow and not
the "l" sound as
in Amarillo, Texas.

Tomorrow's word is *arroz.*

Rice is linked conceptually
to *Arroyo*, or dry river.
They both need *agua* to exist.

How confused I was when a teacher
explained how much water it takes
to grow rice; newspapers confused me too:
arroz grew in Vietnam,
the Arroyos grew in Chicago.

Name Giveaway

PHIL GEORGE

. . . . . .

That teacher gave me a new name . . . again.
She never even had feasts or a giveaway!

Still I do not know what "George" means;
and now she calls me "Phillip."

TWO FLOCKS OF GEESE LIGHTING UPON
STILL WATERS
must be a name too hard to remember.

Faggot

THOMAS SAYERS ELLIS

. . . . . .

We nicknamed Robert
Robin because he played
With girls and memorized cheers,
Preferred Home Economics to Shop.

In Gym he switched like them
And could control his strength,
Hitting volleyballs with his wrist
To boys of his choice.

Like somebody's sister,
He rolled his eyes and fought
With his hands open, backing away,
Kicking & scratching, a windmill of self-defense.

For this we called him punk,
Faggot, sissy, whistling & kissing,
Whenever Miss Williams left the classroom
Or turned to write on the board.

In talent shows he sang "Baby Love"
Backed by girls we had crushes on,
Signifying he knew more about
The opposite sex than us.

He did. We were virgins.
Our big brothers protected him,
Saying we'd understand when
The fuzzy shadows under our arms

And between our legs
Turned to hair. When one
Of our rubber bands bruised his neck,
His father came to school

and beat the shit out of him,
Erasing our passion
Mark with marks
Of his own.

Definitions

BARBARA CLEARY

. . . . . .

In Bridgeport, tough kids smirked at words:
Emerson's *Diadem. Faggot.*
At recess, their steel-toed shoes
surrounded smaller boys
in chain-link playground.
Rachel sat in the front row
barely moving, silencing
her silver charm bracelet
against her classmates' din.
Her small dark eyes met mine,
connecting meanings,
collecting images,
from the list of Latin-rooted syllables.
And Carla — usually absent on vocabulary days —
got pregnant that year.
She said it happened in my cloakroom
at Black Rock School
when she and Ricky went to get their books
for vocab review
and never came back.

The Spelling-Bee as Foreshadowing

CAROLE OLES

· · · · ·

The auditorium swallowed
contenders alive
while the whole student body
was made to endure
Miss Riegel pronouncing the words
like life-terms.

We knew what was important:
arranging letters
like workclothes on a line.
I before *E* was order we could
count on. We knew
the maverick *weird*.

To be grade-school champ
I spelled *impeccable*,
a dashing stranger.
An angel bent to my ear
and whispered "Double *c*!"

In the citywide finals
I was tasting the win
when the judge gave me *fuchsia*.

Where was my angel
to warn of the snake,
the sly *s*?
What was the rule?

Later I looked up the word
and stared long
at that showy, pendant, crimson,
unspellable flower.

Spelling

JEANNE SHANNON

. . . . . .

Right in the middle of the geography lesson about coal mining
in Virginia and Kentucky, Mr. Collins calls on Larry Bledsoe to
spell "bituminous." "B-i-t-u" Larry starts out, then hesitates,
then draws a deep breath and goes on: "n-i-m-u-s." Well, Lord,
that's not right, Rhoda Sue Rasnick mutters, the minute before
Mr. Collins calls on *her* to spell it. She sails right through, like
she always does. It's hard to find a word in the geography book—
or any other book—that she can't spell. Next he calls on Gaynelle
Bates to spell "anthracite," and then has to call on two more
pupils before Jimmy Ray Blankenship gets it right. Now that
we're through with the spelling part, he's asking us what's the
difference between bituminous and anthracite coal, and which
kind does Southwest Virginia have. He doesn't say, "What kind of
coal does your daddy mine?" He used to talk about our daddies
working in the coal mines, but he doesn't anymore. Not since
Rhoda Sue's daddy was killed in a slate fall at Number 9 Jenkins
across the mountain in Kentucky, the week before her baby
brother was born.

Yuba City School

CHITRA BANERJEE DIVAKARUNI

. . . . . .

From the black trunk I shake out
my one American skirt, blue serge
that smells of mothballs. Again today
Neeraj came crying from school. All week
the teacher has made him sit
in the last row, next to the fat boy
who drools and mumbles,
picks at the spotted milk-blue
skin of his face, but knows
to pinch, sudden-sharp,
when she is not looking.

The books are full of black curves,
dots like the eggs the boll-weevil laid
each monsoon in the furniture-cracks
in Ludhiana. Far up in front
the teacher makes word-sounds
Neeraj does not know. They float
from her mouth-cave, he says,
in discs, each a different color.

Learning to Read

THOMAS R. SMITH

. . . . . .

How tired the elbows grew,
bones thrusting against skin.
Flesh took the brunt,
pressed into the carved desk.

In front of the room, a woman —
old, pretty, ugly, young,
she was ours and we were
hers. We hoped for kindness.

Around us, other faces in that
same balance of anticipation
and dread. Large black letters
floated unanchored on the page.

The boy and girl in the pictures looked
friendly, but only those who could
fit the sounds into words
were allowed to join their play.

The ones who couldn't learn
smoldered with a fatal resentment
I rarely noticed before it gushed
a bloody nose on the playground.

Meanwhile my mind turned a word,
grasped it, used it as a key
to open the door to a refuge
beyond hard desks and fists.

How Grammar School Is Changing

MAURICE KILWEIN GUEVARA

In the early years all of the teachers were Nouns. They were very strict Nouns. They wore black robes that reached to the floor and had a fondness for caning the palms of your hands. In the beginning there was very little light; then a window was placed in the east wall of the school. The first Verb to enter the classroom through our new and only window was a Be. It was yellow and black and buzzed by my ear. One day Be walked vertically up the world map from Santiago to Santa Marta and stopped to smell the salt water. Thinking twice, it flew up to Florida and was eyeing Orange County when my mean third grade Noun squashed Be with her big white reader. She said, "We only need one river in this town," which didn't make any sense. It wasn't long, however, before more stuff started coming in through the windows (there were soon four) and through the new fire doors and down the chimney: Adjectives with big, bright, yellow and orange, polka-dot bow ties; Adverbs who yodeled longingly for their homeland; a Pronoun who wore cornrows with green ribbons (I confess I had my first crush on She); a family of Silver Brackets; Question Marks and Periods snowed down the chimney; and, finally, the Invisible Etceteras—pranksters that they are—started moaning sweet nothings in my Noun's ear, which made her grin a little, thank God. By the time I was in the fifth grade, after a vicious fight with the village elders, the principal had hired Dr. Miguel de Sustantivo to make the school bilingual: *y tú sabes lo que pasó después: vinieron las familias Adjetivo y Pronombre y Verbo y más y más. . . .* But yesterday a new little someone came from far, far away who sits sad all alone at lunch. Does anyone know a few words in Vietnamese? I would like to say Good Morning.

Penmanship

JORIE GRAHAM

. . . . . .

Beyond the margin, in the mind, the winner gets it right,
while here the *l*'s proceed in single file,
each a large or smaller eye.
What heaven can be true
when its permissions
vary so? The page

is turned. Try it again. Each page a new decor, as here
the *f*'s so many shut umbrellas on
an empty beach, the waves the *s*'s make unable to link up,
reach shore, and this
a greenhouse, rows and rows and I
can't ever pick
the one I want,

and this desert we'd reclaim,

and these the flooded lowlands, topsoil gone downstream,
    the ocean
flashing her green garments, many-stemmed and
many-headed,

and this our frigid school of twenty-six now swimming up
stream, swimming down, made to try
and try again,

and oh their desire, one by one, is for normalcy, marriage,
these labials and gutturals narrowing their aim,
shedding the body for
its wish, a pure idea, a thought as true as
not true, water

lilies, water-
striders . . .

Catatonia

In a Classroom for the Slow to Learn

CLENN REED

. . . . . .

Jason, look at this book, I say,
but feel like I'm in a dream he's having,
a ship at anchor off the island he is
that dispenses words like boats to his shore.
He knows better than to talk.

So then, I ask: *Jason, do you like to read?*
and lift the cover, letting a few
pages flip between us—water lapping
onto small stones. His thin fingers
jitter uncontrollably on the desk.

Caught here, with heckles of children
filling the blurred world behind us,
I'm looking for a key to unlock
this tongue squirreled into a mute nest.
Where's the cure that's always close at hand?

What am I here, on this edge
where senses never get sorted out,
too large for the chair I'm sitting in
before a boy whose eyes, like brown leaves
blown into white cups, will not look at mine?

Why would a stranger place himself
where nobody was before and speak? A bright
winter sky slides across rectangular panes—sharp
light. *Jason,* I say, and *Jason,* again,
then turn and head back out to sea.

Rain

NAOMI SHIHAB NYE

. . . . . .

A teacher asked Paul
what he would remember
from third grade, and he sat
a long time before writing
"this year sumbody tutched me
on the sholder"
and turned his paper in.
Later she showed it to me
as an example of her wasted life.
The words he wrote were large
as houses in a landscape.
He wanted to go inside them
and live, he could fill in
the windows of "o" and "d"
and be safe while outside
birds building nests in drainpipes
knew nothing of the coming rain.

Reaching to a Sky of Soba

DAVID HASSLER

. . . . . .

I walk past winter boots lined up in rows,
through the door: Ms. Brown's ten o'clock 5-A English.
The students crowd around.
They want to know how tall I am
and if my hair is real.
I hold out my hands to measure their heads.
A stranger in their room, I stand near
a small stool they call the author's chair.
Snow falls outside, beyond
windows dressed with pilgrim hats and turkeys.
Reading my poem, "Eating Soba,"
I say poetry lets you talk to things
you don't normally talk to, and
here, I'm talking to noodles,
as though my bowl were a smiling friend.
In Japan, you can slurp as loud
as you want. The louder,
the greater the compliment to the chef.
The class practices slurping.
One boy asks,
Could you say the sky is a bowl of soba?
I smile, yes!
Then the sun is a raw egg floating in it!
Another hand appears.
Trees are chopsticks.
Heads turn to look out the windows.
And clouds are steam rising above.
The students gasp and applaud.
Planets are onions.
The moon is a bump at the bottom of the bowl.
Earthquakes break up the noodles, their rumbling is slurping.
Our mouths are Black Holes breathing it in.
God is the chef.
Meteors are coins we throw down to pay.

Then the shy boy, looking at the floor, raises his hand.
The universe is a giant bowl of soba.
We keep eating and eating until the last explosion.
When the universe ends, he says, *our bowl is empty.*
The bell rings, their hands still reaching in the air.

Advice to Young Writers

RON PADGETT

. . . . . .

One of the things I've repeated to writing
students is that they should write when they don't
feel like writing, just sit down and start,
and when it doesn't go very well, to press on then,
to get to that one thing you'd otherwise
never find. What I forgot to mention was
that this is just a writing technique, that
you could also be out mowing the lawn, where
if you bring your mind to it, you'll also eventually
come to something unexpected ("The robin he
hunts and pecks"), or watching the FARM NEWS
on which a large man is referring to the "Greater
Massachusetts area." It's alright, students, not
to write. Do whatever you want. As long as you find
that unexpected something, or even if you don't.

Ode

THOMAS CENTOLELLA

. . . . . .

You want them to write
an ode, a love song
to whatever delights
or defines them, and all they want
is to mock the drone
of the math teacher stuck in the fifties,
whose pants are too short and socks
are white. Or they want
to rattle off the slang
for their greatest curse,
their favorite sport:
the body parts that possess them
and which they yearn to possess,
the latest secret code of sex
they figure you can't decipher.
Or they want, simply,
to be left alone. Look
at this one, huddled inside
his arctic hood, asleep and slumped
toward the open window, explorer
of the other way. Or this one,
who recoils from being made
to speak the little she loves
for fear it will vanish, as so much
already has by her sixteenth year.
You too are afraid: that you don't have
what it takes to touch them
the way they need to be touched,
which is why you want them
to do for themselves, praise
whatever sustains them, whatever
is good and doesn't go away.
And so, how can you not love them
when they answer with anti-odes:

to homework and take-homes,
to slow death by boredom, to the unspeakable
acts their bodies have endured for years
and for which they are only beginning
to find the pathetic and necessary words?
And on your last day, how can you
not love it when the quietest one
is changing at his locker
in a crowded hallway, teasing
the girls as he drops his pants,
the girls pretending they're in shock,
how can you hear him sing,
almost to himself, *I'm the one*
you love to hate—young boy smile
on a young man face, the old joy
of self-love still intact—how can you
hear him sing and not want to sing along,
not want to smile back?

Learning Spanish

SARA GOODRICH

. . . . . .

I did not want to learn Spanish.
I hated the way
the words spilled out lazily
from my teacher's lips
like sleepy dogs,
even though English is unwieldy,
and sometimes,
consonants get jammed.

Spanish used to come like English,
only worse.
I choked on *dieciocho* and *abuelito*.
I swallowed double *r*'s
and pronounced them
like I was from North Carolina.

But I have never had a language before
that tasted like horse
and felt like marshmallows.
I say things like:
La mesa con pollo, blanquios, calcuadora,
compra la radio y quiero ir afeitarse
a la casa anaranjado, for the Hell of it.
I still can't say *anaranjado*
without running out of breath.

I listen to my Mexican friends,
jealous and relieved.

When I speak Spanish,
I am much older—

maybe an old woman
about to die
spinning prayers like cotton,
and fading
into something like sand.

Lecciones de la Lengua, 1970

BRENDA CÁRDENAS

. . . . . .

She is proud of her papá
because he comes
to their little grey school,
converted from army barracks,
to teach Español
to Mrs. Benda's fifth grade.
And that means they don't
have to listen to that awful
Amelia Weiss on t.v.
with her screech owl version
of "Las Mañanitas" and her annoying
forefinger to the ear,
    "Escuchen"
and then to the lips,
    "y repitan."

He teaches them to order
Coca-Cola en el restaurán—
    Señor, quisiera una Coca, por favor—
and the names of all the utensils—
    cuchara, cuchillo, tenedor.
The children look at him funny
when he picks up the knife.
Next week he will show
the bullfights he watched
in Mexico when he was *muy chiquitito.*
He will choose a boy to snort, stomp, charge
the red cloth that he'll snap at his side
as he dodges the sharp-horned strike,
stabs invisible swords
into the boy's hide

and makes the children laugh.

How My Father Learned English

JULIA KASDORF

. . . . . .

Breathing his own breath,
forehead pressed in a corner
while the teacher's syllables
pelted his back, meaningless.
At some point, he says, it just
began to make sense, sounds gave
up significance as neatly
as the clear and yolk slipped
into batter when his mother tapped
a bowl and pulled eggshells apart.
How could she bear to think
of her first-grader, mute and confused
the long season from Labor Day
to Christmas, begging translation
from desk mates, pestering hired men
for names of things during chores?
She knew he'd eventually piece together
a tongue with words from home
and school. Only this fall I think
to ask how that happened, though
I've taught English for years,
eagerly asking the foreigners
to tell me about their homes,
Please, I urge, say it in English.

3 / A History of Our People

The History Teacher

BILLY COLLINS

· · · · ·

Trying to protect his students' innocence
he told them the Ice Age was really just
the Chilly Age, a period of a million years
when everyone had to wear sweaters.

And the Stone Age became the Gravel Age,
named after the long driveways of the time.

The Spanish Inquisition was nothing more
than an outbreak of questions such as
"How far is it from here to Madrid?"
"What do you call the matador's hat?"

The War of the Roses took place in a garden,
and the Enola Gay dropped one tiny atom
on Japan.

The children would leave his classroom
for the playground to torment the weak
and the smart,
mussing up their hair and breaking their glasses,

while he gathered up his notes and walked home
past flower beds and white picket fences,
wondering if they would believe that soldiers
in the Boer War told long, rambling stories
designed to make the enemy nod off.

Nostalgia

JOYCE CAROL OATES

. . . . . .

Rural District School # 7, Ransomville, New York

Crumbling stone steps of the old schoolhouse
Boarded-up windows   shards of winking glass
Built 1898, numerals faint in stone as shadow
Through a window, obedient rows of desks   mute
Only a droning of hornets beneath the eaves,
the cries of red-winged blackbirds by the creek

How many generations of this rocky countryside grown & gone
How many memories   & all forgotten
no one to chronicle, no regret

& the schoolhouse soon to be razed   & goodbye to America
The flagless pole, what a relief!
I love it, the eye lifting skyward   to nothing
Never to pledge allegiance to the United States of America again
Never to press my flat right hand over my heart again as if I had one

Drill, 1957

NANCE VAN WINCKEL

. . . . . .

If we could angle the sunbeam of the song
through our bent bones, we might sparkle ourselves

out of here. If we could lift our foreheads
from the bricks, our knees from the floor,

we might shut down the claxon, stop its deep
irredeemable ache. How long can we do this

before a real thing happens — this filing out,
this kneeling fast, hands up over our heads.

We know the way to make ourselves sunbeams,
even though the teacher paces behind us,

ordering our heads lower, even though
the cold comes rumbling through the bricks

and through my most secret silent voice,
which can never hit the high notes

sweet enough. This prayerful pose
is a lie. It just makes trouble.

We've seen what they think they're hiding —
the overgrown shadows with the overgrown heads.

They follow us out and huddle just over
our own. We get only someone's word for this.

Patience. They call it a practice
for patience. But who can be sure of a bell

so big? Or figure a real sunbeam: what it was
before it was dust, before it was struck through with light.

Soul Make a Path through Shouting

CYRUS CASSELLS

. . . . . .

for Elizabeth Eckford   Little Rock, Arkansas, 1957

Thick at the schoolgate are the ones
Rage has twisted
Into minotaurs, harpies
Relentlessly swift;
So you must walk past the pincers,
The swaying horns,
Sister, sister,
Straight through the gusts
Of fear and fury,
Straight through:
Where are you going?

I'm just going to school.

Here we go to meet
The hydra-headed day,
Here we go to meet
The maelstrom —

Can my voice be an angel-on-the-spot,
An amen corner?
Can my voice take you there,
Gallant girl with a notebook,
Up, up from the shadows of gallows trees
To the other shore:
A globe bathed in light,
A chalkboard blooming with equations —

I have never seen the likes of you,
Pioneer in dark glasses:
You won't show the mob your eyes,
But I know your gaze,
Steady-on-the-North-Star, burning—

With their jerry-rigged faith,
Their spear of the American flag,
How could they dare to believe
You're someone sacred?:
Nigger, burr-headed girl,
Where are you going?

I'm just going to school.

Janes Avenue

DICK ALLEN

. . . . . .

At the end of it, the school
that was once a museum: stairs from its second floor
led up to a huge locked door
and the reek, we imagined, of the missing mummy.

Get down from there,
our teachers — sad Depression things —
would shout. But we kept trying,
small shoulders pushing; hands on the pitted black knob.

They lied it wasn't there. We knew
as sure as we knew rowboats, wind and clouds,
in that cupola room, propped on a broken desk,
a mummy stood in brown-stained strips of cloth.

We hated them for lying. Oh, we knew, we knew
when the last bell sent us home, they gathered
by the door; the Principal unlocked it;
they entered and they gazed and they were shaken.

As we wished to be. The frogs that spewed
beneath our bicycles, the horseflies in the grass —
these were the small things they thought fit for us,
the happy children of Janes Avenue.

Lunch

MARC HARSHMAN

. . . . . .

"Bumblebees,"
Mom guessed, rightly,
were macaroni and cheese,
a meal
not yet tasted
in this not quite yet modern world,
and for which, without TV,
I found no other words
with which to name my exotic meal.

The mashed potatoes dressed with egg noodles,
fried chicken, baked steak, ham loaf,
fresh beans and stewed tomatoes,
creamed peas and onions,
pies and cakes and cobblers,
occurred only the first year,
no cafeteria, only volunteers,
our farming mothers to see us fed
the old foods, the old ways.

Later, the flavor of milk
left to live within paraffin
and cardboard —
not quite sour
not quite milk.

How Steel Shapes Our Lives

Grade Two, Arlington Elementary

JEANNE BRYNER

. . . . .

Our teacher, Mrs. Dillon, raises
the square white screen.
It might be a sail wanting wind
or our mothers' pale sheets
trying to dry in January.

This is Ohio. 1958.
This, our third year away from West Virginia
and the forsythia by the farmhouse.
This is assembly: gray chairs, a movie,
about *How Steel Shapes Our Lives.*
We are small, our hands folded.

Mornings of walking with my grandfather
to the barn are far away.
Still, lambs crying for dead mothers
must be bottle fed. I know it
and know how, when they suck,
it feels good to pet their wet faces.

Mr. Jonah makes the room go dark,
then, he flips a switch: magic, magic.
A light warms the reel's black film,
upside-down numbers flash. We hear
a big voice without a face.

We have been taught to sit and listen.
The movie makes us feel like we're beside
the men in hard hats, where yellow dozers
gouge the earth, take what they want,
haul it to our mills for processing.

This is the inside of a steel mill, the voice says.
We watch the men move like shadows on the screen.
These are the stories given to children:
evil trolls beneath the bridge, to cross over
someone must pay a toll or be eaten.

This is a blast furnace, the big voice says.
We don't even know what that means, but
a pink glow settles on our faces
as the ladle vomits its river of red steel.
Sparks spray the mens' coveralls, hands,
and hair—men who look like Tom's father,

Debbie's father, my father, so I whisper
Run, Run, Run, and rub my Bible-school
Jesus pin for luck. But, there's so much noise
in the mill, the men can't hear me.
They wear their iron shoes
and keep walking through the fire.

Public School 190, Brooklyn 1963

MARTÍN ESPADA

. . . . . .

The inkwells had no ink.
The flag had 48 stars, four years
after Alaska and Hawaii.
There were vandalized blackboards
and chairs with three legs,
taped windows, retarded boys penned
in the basement.
Some of us stared in Spanish.
We windmilled punches
or hid in the closet to steal from coats
as the teacher drowsed, head bobbing.
We had the Dick and Jane books,
but someone filled in their faces
with a brown crayon.

When Kennedy was shot,
they hurried us onto buses,
not saying why,
saying only that
something bad had happened.
But we knew
something bad had happened,
knew that before
November 22, 1963.

Sunglasses

Air Raid Drill at Wildwood Elementary, November 22, 1963

DAVID WOJAHN

. . . . . .

We snake in single file down the hall,
Child stars and starlets sporting shades,
To the basement lunchroom where we'll huddle,
Condemned to silence, ten minutes with our heads

Between our legs. *And if you sense a flash,*
I don't want you to look at it. Miss Bloom
Counts down the minutes, flicks the light switch
On and off. Then footsteps click across the room.

Whispers, and we file back upstairs
Without the films on hygiene or the wicked Reds.
Murmurs from every desk. Miss Bloom's in tears,
Her makeup streaks. Miss Bloom collects our shades.

Daylight presses in. The loudspeaker
Coughs on, the static bristling like gunfire.

Plum-Dark Humor

MAURICE KILWEIN GUEVARA

. . . . . .

David teaches history to children. Today,
he is showing them a film of the war
in Vietnam. "America," he explains,
"was defending the South," as he watches
what he'd seen as a child from the living room floor.
Some of the children have decided to put their heads
down. And David doesn't feel well
sitting in the small chair.

Two images are clearest in his mind:
the naked girl on fire, running,
and this man, hands bound behind him,
being pushed, a small crowd nearby.
Another person, khaki uniform, holding a gun,
enters into view, waves the people back with his pistol,
fires into the man's brain and, bent,
the man falls sideways. Blood pumps and flows
warmly from his temple, oozes, slows,
forming a puddle on the dried-mud road.
David feels dizzy, tries to turn the projector off,
but instead switches the control to REVERSE.

And the dead man's mind draws
the blood back in, and the corpse flies up,
straightening out, and stands as instantly
the wound heals; the murderer waves the crowd on,
walking backwards out of the picture.

Some of the children are laughing.

Spitting in the Leaves

MAGGIE ANDERSON

In Spanishburg there are boys in tight jeans,
mud on their cowboy boots and they wear huge hats
with feathers, skunk feathers they tell me.
They do not want to be in school, but are.
Some teacher cared enough to hold them. Unlike
their thin disheveled cousins, the boys on Matoaka's
Main Street in October who loll against parking meters
and spit into the leaves. Because of them, someone
will think we need a war, will think the best solution
would be for them to take their hats and feathers,
their good country manners and drag them off somewhere,
to Vietnam, to El Salvador. And they'll go.
They'll go from West Virginia, from hills and back roads
that twist like politics through trees, and they'll fight,
not because they know what for but because what they know
is how to fight. What they know is feathers,
their strong skinny arms, their spitting
in the leaves.

Indian Boarding School

The Runaways

LOUISE ERDRICH

. . . . . .

Home's the place we head for in our sleep.
Boxcars stumbling north in dreams
don't wait for us. We catch them on the run.
The rails, old lacerations that we love,
shoot parallel across the face and break
just under Turtle Mountains. Riding scars
you can't get lost. Home is the place they cross.

The lame guard strikes a match and makes the dark
less tolerant. We watch through cracks in boards
as the land starts rolling, rolling till it hurts
to be here, cold in regulation clothes.
We know the sheriff's waiting at midrun
to take us back. His car is dumb and warm.
The highway doesn't rock, it only hums
like a wing of long insults. The worn-down welts
of ancient punishments lead back and forth.

All runaways wear dresses, long green ones,
the color you would think shame was. We scrub
the sidewalks down because it's shameful work.
Our brushes cut the stone in watered arcs
and in the soak frail outlines shiver clear
a moment, things us kids pressed on the dark
face before it hardened, pale, remembering
delicate old injuries, the spines of names and leaves.

The Grade School I Attended
Was Next to a Slaughterhouse

CHRIS LLEWELLYN

. . . . . .

How do you like to go up in a swing,
Up in the air so blue?
Oh, I do think it the pleasantest thing
Ever a child can do!
—Robert Louis Stevenson

My feet pass cupola, weathercock,
touch nimbus clouds over Holmes
School. Chainsaw spurt-squeals,
pigs screaming, I know I must
go higher to make these rusty
swingchains outshout death.

*

Too scared for sex, so my beau
pumped me standing up in swings.
April sprang its stars over
Holmes School, the animals asleep,
we hummed in chains.

Busing

JAMES HARMS

. . . . . .

Pasadena, California, 1974

Fog sifts through the rising light.
A block away a school bus shimmers
driving through water, and I sit
on the curb like a bubble waiting
to rise. If my sister is with me
there are two of us, two quiet
white kids, our friends from the block
melting away as the bus gets closer,
until it's just me and her, remnants
of a neighborhood that isn't here anymore.
There are never any seats left for us
on the bus, though there are plenty
of empty seats, and my sister will now
and then sit on a black girl's books
or cuss at her, sounding exactly like
what she doesn't look like, sounding short
and black. But she's tall, too tall for any girl
to try. And she says, "Sit down, Jimmy,
just sit on their hands," while I stare up
the aisle, past the driver's swiveling head,
and stand. I try not to fall as the bus rocks
down the street, try not to end up in someone's
lap, someone who, for as long as it takes
to get to school, hates me. Outside
the backdrop changes; we move from city
to suburb. A boy looks up at me, his hair
squeezed into a net and shiny with vaseline.
I know him from class, where he never breathes
a word. Not even when Mr. Moore spreads
his fingers on the desk and leans out

over the first row saying, "It's OK
to be wrong, let's just try." But we know
it's OK. I look at the boy and smile.
He looks away. Being wrong
is what we have in common.

Bully

MARTÍN ESPADA

. . . . . .

Boston, Massachusetts, 1987

In the school auditorium
the Theodore Roosevelt statue
is nostalgic
for the Spanish-American War,
each fist lonely for a saber
or the reins of anguish-eyed horses,
or a podium to clatter with speeches
glorying in the malaria of conquest.

But now the Roosevelt school
is pronounced *Hernández.*
Puerto Rico has invaded Roosevelt
with its army of Spanish-singing children
in the hallways,
brown children devouring
the stockpiles of the cafeteria,
children painting *Taíno* ancestors
that leap naked across murals.

Roosevelt is surrounded
by all the faces
he ever shoved in eugenic spite
and cursed as mongrels, skin of one race,
hair and cheekbones of another.

Once Marines tramped
from the newsreel of his imagination;
now children plot to spray graffiti
in parrot-brilliant colors
across the Victorian mustache
and monocle.

St. Peter Claver

TOI DERRICOTTE

. . . . . .

Every town with black Catholics has a St. Peter Claver's.
My first was nursery school.
Miss Maturin made us fold our towels in a regulation square
    and nap on army cots.
No mother questioned; no child sassed.
In blue pleated skirts, pants, and white shirts,
we stood in line to use the open toilets
and conserved light by walking in darkness.
Unsmiling, mostly light-skinned, we were the children of the middle
    class, preparing to take our parents' places in a world that would
    demand we fold our hands and wait.
They said it was good for us, the bowl of soup, its pasty whiteness;
I learned to swallow and distrust my senses.

On holy cards St. Peter's face is olive-toned, his hair near kinky;
I thought he was one of us who pass between the rich and poor,
    the light and dark.
Now I read he was "a Spanish Jesuit priest who labored for
    the salvation of the African Negroes and the abolition
    of the slave trade."
I was tricked again, robbed of my patron,
and left with a debt to another white man.

Barbie Says Math Is Hard

KYOKO MORI

. . . . .

As a boy, I'd still have asked
why Jack must spend exactly
two dollars at the corner store.
Give him a coin purse is as
good an answer as five apples
and two oranges. Also: would
he bake the apples into pies
or cobblers, save the orange peel
in glass jars to spice up his
tea or cake? If his father
paints their house with Mr. Jones,
which man will take the peaks and
why? Would the raspberry beetles
swarm over wet paint? Why is
Mr. Jones slower than his
neighbor? If x equals y,
is it like putting apples into
cole slaw the way a tomato
is really a fruit? None of my
dolls talked or grew hair. In
third grade, Satsuki and I
traded our Barbies' limbs so
mine could flex her left biceps
while hers sat cross-legged
raising one stiff arm
like a weapon. If Satsuki has
daughters, she might remember
the grasshoppers we caught,
how we cupped two hands together
into crooked globes to
hear them rattling inside like
a small motor. She would tell
her daughters: Yes, math was hard,
but not because we were girls.

A History of Sexual Preference

ROBIN BECKER

. . . . . .

We are walking our very public attraction
through eighteenth-century Philadelphia.
I am simultaneously butch girlfriend
and suburban child on a school trip,
Independence Hall, 1775, home
to the Second Continental Congress.
Although she is wearing her leather jacket,
although we have made love for the first time
in a hotel room on Rittenhouse Square,
I am preparing my teenage escape from Philadelphia,
from Elfreth's Alley, the oldest continuously occupied
residential street in the nation,
from Carpenters' Hall, from Congress Hall,
from Graff House where the young Thomas
Jefferson lived, summer of 1776. In my starched shirt
and waistcoat, in my leggings and buckled shoes,
in postmodern drag, as a young eighteenth-century statesman,
I am seventeen and tired of fighting for freedom
and the rights of men. I am already dreaming of Boston—
city of women, demonstrations, and revolution
on a grand and personal scale.
                              Then the maître d'
is pulling out our chairs for brunch, we have the
surprised look of people who have been kissing
and now find themselves dressed and dining
in a Locust Street townhouse turned café,
who do not know one another very well, who continue
with optimism to pursue relationship. *Eternity*
may simply be our mortal default mechanism
set on *hope* despite all evidence. In this mood,
I roll up my shirtsleeves and she touches my elbow.
I refuse the seedy view from the hotel window.
I picture instead their silver inkstands,
the hoopskirt factory on Arch Street,

the Wireworks, their eighteenth-century herb gardens,
their nineteenth-century row houses restored
with period door knockers.
Step outside.
We have been deeded the largest landscaped space
within a city anywhere in the world. In Fairmount Park,
on horseback, among the ancient ginkoes, oaks, persimmons,
and magnolias, we are seventeen and imperishable, cutting classes
May of our senior year. And I am happy as the young
Tom Jefferson, unbuttoning my collar, imagining his power,
considering my healthy body, how I might use it in the service
of the country of my pleasure.

Day-Tripping

ALLISON JOSEPH

. . . . . .

In that dark classroom,
we watched frame after frame
of antidrug filmstrips,
cartoons some genius invented
to scare us straight,
keep us from mind-blowing
temptations, each gaudy scene
chronicling the adventures
of some poor animated sap
who couldn't resist the stranger
who sidled up to him
on the playground, offering
handfuls of tiny glossy
blue and red pills. Stupid fool,
he thought they were candy,
swallowed them easily,
tossing uppers into his mouth,
his big cartoon character head
swelling as he took off
on his two wheeler,
trying to fly, pumping the pedals
faster and faster, only to careen
into a white garden gate,
a scenario someone somewhere
thought would scare us.
But the blond fool on his toy bike
only set us to laughing,
giggles erupting all around
the room, our teacher
demanding quiet, refusing
to move that fine little film
forward until we shut up.
By the time we hushed,
Blondie was back at the

playground, his friend
from the day before back again
dressed in the same platform shoes,
wide lapels, bell-bottoms.
Something to calm you down,
he whispered, leaning in
to put eight nine ten pills
in the little idiot's hands.
He stuffed them all down,
walked home to mother and dad
only to fall asleep
over family dinner,
dreaming into his mashed potatoes.
Mother was shocked, but knew
it was drugs, and when her boy
came to, they hugged,
their big cartoony mouths
open wide to warn us
about strange men who offer
pretty candies to boys and girls.
Turning the film off,
the lights back on,
our teacher asked *any questions*
now that you've stopped laughing,
her face severe, unsmiling,
arms crossed rigid
over her bony chest,
and Kevin, sprawled in the back row,
sneakers up on my desk,
slurred, *Where can I find me a man*
who won't make me pay nothin'
for all the shit I want?

Fears of the Eighth Grade

TOI DERRICOTTE

. . . . . .

When I ask what things they fear,
their arms raise like soldiers volunteering for battle:
Fear of going into a dark room, my murderer is waiting.
Fear of taking a shower, someone will stab me.
Fear of being kidnapped, raped.
Fear of dying in war.
When I ask how many fear this,
all the children raise their hands.

I think of this little box of consecrated land,
the bombs somewhere else,
the dead children in their mothers' arms,
women crying at the gates of the bamboo palace.

How thin the veneer!
The paper towels, napkins, toilet paper—everything
burned up in a day.

These children see the city after Armageddon.
The demons stand visible in the air
between their friends talking.
They see fire in a spring day
the instant before conflagration.
They feel blood through closed faucets,
the dead rising from the boiling seas.

Among Children

PHILIP LEVINE

. . . . . .

I walk among the rows of bowed heads—
the children are sleeping through fourth grade
so as to be ready for what is ahead,
the monumental boredom of junior high
and the rush forward tearing their wings
loose and turning their eyes forever inward.
These are the children of Flint, their fathers
work at the spark plug factory or truck
bottled water in 5 gallon sea-blue jugs
to the widows of the suburbs. You can see
already how their backs have thickened,
how their small hands, soiled by pig iron,
leap and stutter even in dreams. I would like
to sit down among them and read slowly
from *The Book of Job* until the windows
pale and the teacher rises out of a milky sea
of industrial scum, her gowns streaming
with light, her foolish words transformed
into song, I would like to arm each one
with a quiver of arrows so that they might
rush like wind there where no battle rages
shouting among the trumpets, Ha! Ha!
How dear the gift of laughter in the face
of the 8 hour day, the cold winter mornings
without coffee and oranges, the long lines
of mothers in old coats waiting silently
where the gates have closed. Ten years ago
I went among these same children, just born,
in the bright ward of the Sacred Heart and leaned
down to hear their breaths delivered that day,
burning with joy. There was such wonder
in their sleep, such purpose in their eyes
closed against autumn, in their damp heads
blurred with the hair of ponds, and not one

turned against me or the light, not one
said, I am sick, I am tired, I will go home,
not one complained or drifted alone,
unloved, on the hardest day of their lives.
Eleven years from now they will become
the men and women of Flint or Paradise,
the majors of a minor town, and I
will be gone into smoke or memory,
so I bow to them here and whisper
all I know, all I will never know.

4 / Recess

Autobiographia Literaria
FRANK O'HARA

. . . . . .

When I was a child
I played by myself in a
corner of the schoolyard
all alone.

I hated dolls and I
hated games, animals were
not friendly and birds
flew away.

If anyone was looking
for me I hid behind a
tree and cried out "I am
an orphan."

And here I am, the
center of all beauty!
writing these poems!
Imagine!

Stayed Back

THOMAS SAYERS ELLIS

. . . . . .

All the schools I attended
Were enormous, within walking distance
Of home, public. An A and B student,
I didn't start messing up until
My senior year. Cynthia Jones,

Who taught us Literature,
Warned me first: stop staying out
So late! But, that young, everything
Worth knowing had to be experienced
Firsthand, then learned.

In class, drunk on drums,
Too weary to perform, my mind
Was always somewhere else—
The Howard Theatre, Hains Point,
Chasing girls, listening to Go-Go.

Recess was precious, sometimes
Lasting all day like summer. We'd sit in
Victor Sparrow's Deuce & a Quarter
Blasting RARE ESSENCE, doors open,
Legs hanging—bent like broken wings,

Which is where Kenny MaGhee
Found me, outside Dunbar, perpetrating
And pretending I knew the timbales.
Ambition—no, a lie—cost me a year.
Also brought me closer to verse, here.

Schoolyard in April

KENNETH KOCH

. . . . . .

Little girls smearing
the stolen lipstick
of overheard grown-up talk
into their conversation,
unconscious of the beauty
of their movements
like milkweed in the wind,
are beginning to drift
over by the drinking fountain
where they will skip rope

They speak in whispers
about the omnipotent teachers
while the little boys
scoff over their ball-mitts

The teachers themselves
stare out of windows,
remembering April.

Escape

NAOMI SHIHAB NYE

. . . . . .

We raised our hands for the honor of leaving the class—to carry a
message, a coffee can of soiled brushes to the janitor's sink. One
day the door of the janitor's closet banged shut behind us locking
us in with the colors red and blue. Karen, the spindly spineless
one, gripped my arm. A light bulb dangled on a long cord. Jugs
of bleach lined the walls. We called and called, pounding on
the door. Red and blue swirled together in a vanishing purple
stream. I scrawled HELP! on a paper towel, pressing it out under
the crack. But no one passed. If they passed, they didn't look
down. By now the class had gone to recess or they would have
remembered us. Our empty desks. We held hands. Karen
whimpered like a cat. At night the radiators might stop clicking
in the building. There would be no heat. We were terrified, but
we had what we wanted.

Trouble with Math in a
One-Room Country School

JANE KENYON

. . . . . .

The others bent their heads and started in.
Confused, I asked my neighbor
to explain—a sturdy, bright-cheeked girl
who brought raw milk to school from her family's
herd of Holsteins. Ann had a blue bookmark,
and on it Christ revealed His beating heart,
holding the flesh back with His wounded hand.
Ann understood division. . . .

Miss Moran sprang from her monumental desk
and led me roughly through the class
without a word. My shame was radical
as she propelled me past the cloakroom
to the furnace closet, where only the boys
were put, only the older ones at that.
The door swung briskly shut.

The warmth, the gloom, the smell
of sweeping compound clinging to the broom
soothed me. I found a bucket, turned it
upside down, and sat, hugging my knees.
I hummed a theme from Haydn that I knew
from my piano lessons . . .
and hardened my heart against authority.
And then I heard her steps, her fingers
on the latch. She led me, blinking
and changed, back to the class.

Recess

CHRISTOPHER BURSK

. . . . . .

Older boys drag younger by the wrists into woods,
children letting themselves go heavy,
letting themselves sink down inside their shirts.

My son backs against the walls
as if he were watching a brush fire spread toward him,
child by child; he looks away.

In half-empty subways I try not to gaze at coveys of thin boys
touching their hair as if it were on fire,
slicking down the flames.

Boys cursing, blowing smoke in our faces
as if they wanted us to rise
so they could set something else on fire.

As a child I knew I would always be afraid.
My son knows, I see it in his eyes,
in his soft, helpless hands after school.

I hear him in the white light before morning, in his terrible
and unsupervised recesses,
pressed to the wall, crying uncle, uncle.

Beating Up Billy Murphy in Fifth Grade

KATHLEEN AGUERO

. . . . . .

Who knows how it started?
We were the same age, but he was smaller
with wrists you could snap like green beans,
veins that showed blue runners through his skin.
His scalp was like something dead beneath his crewcut
and I hated his pipsqueak voice,
his hanging around with us girls.

Then, somehow, he was face down on the pavement,
my fists banging his back.
When my girlfriends pulled me off,
he whined like a toy engine:
I had hurt his sunburn,
I would pay if he went to the doctor.

He was an orphan I thought I should be nice to.
His aunt planned to send him to military school.
I was ashamed but still sickened
remembering his soft hands, his thin eyelashes,
the schoolgirl in him.

Saving the Crippled Boy

JAN BEATTY

. . . . . .

Tenth-grade field trip, I'm stuck
in the back of the chartered bus
with one-armed Bob Saunders, ten
rows away from the waves of my friends.
There I was, sharing the seat
with his hook of a hand,
his flesh-colored arm-like arm,
was it plastic, what was it made of,
we were sixteen, but it wasn't just
his arm—he was short, his hair
was greasy, he wouldn't talk to anyone.
And who would ever love him, had he ever
kissed a girl—would he ever kiss anyone?
Years before I knew about *mercy fucks*,
somewhere between New York City and Hampton,
it started, and we necked all the way home
from Springdale, the whole time, the bolts
in his arm clicked on the rim of the bus window,
Bob's tongue poking and pushing like
a hyperactive worm in my mouth, me afraid
his arm would flap over me like a hard dead person,
the whole time my good deed burying me, I wanted
to save him, just to save him, and now we were
both alone, covered with our benchwarmers,
Bob half on top of me in the cold vinyl seat,
I felt him get hard—small and hard, and
what had this become, I wanted blazing sanctimony,
saving the crippled boy with each plunge of
my normal tongue, but now I was saying, *Look,
this is what you can't have, not for real,
this is for today*, and I grew small and hard,
and thought of my boyfriend at home, my best
friend, Patty, and my sick, ailing heart.

Catholics

JULIA KASDORF

· · · · · ·

for Julia Lisella

In third grade all the girls got confirmed
and had their ears pierced. They flaunted
those dingy threads that hung from their lobes,
telling how the ice stung, how the cartilage crunched
when the needle broke through, how knots
in the thread had to be pulled through the holes,
one each day, like a prayer on the rosary.

At recess I turned the rope
while Michelle skipped and spun and counted to ten,
and a scapular leapt from the neck of her dress.
She dangled that pale pink ribbon,
a picture of the Blessed Mother on one end
and the Sacred Heart on the other,
saying, "This is my protection, front and back."
That was when I called them Catholic
and said, "Your people killed my people;
your priests threw a man into a river,
tied in a sack with a dog, a cat, a rooster, a snake,
think how they scratched and bit going down,
think how they drowned. Your priests
burned holes in the tongues of our preachers,
and put pacifists naked in cages
to starve and rot while the birds
pecked off their flesh."

Michelle and Vicki and Lisa just looked at me,
the jump rope slack as a snake
at our feet. But in my memory
I want these girls with fine bones and dark eyes
to speak up:
     those priests were not me,
     those martyrs weren't you,

and we have our martyr stories, too.
I want to take their slim girl-bodies into my arms
and tell them I said it only because
I wanted to wear a small, oval medal
I could pull from my T-shirt to kiss
before tests. I wanted a white communion dress,
and to pray with you
to your beautiful Blessed Mother in blue.

The Beating

T. R. HUMMER

. . . . . .

Everybody knew Clifton Cockerell was not half bright,
But nobody knew his passion
Till we found him on the playground back of the junior high
Carving names on a tree. His poor secret
Stood no more chance of staying one

Once we had it, than Clifton did of knowing
Why we cared — but we couldn't let it rest
Till everybody heard it, especially the girl, who was pretty
And thought he was some brand of animal. We'd sing
Their names together every chance we got, impressed

With her way of changing color, like some
Exotic lizard trying to disappear,
And forgot about Clifton pretty much till he came on us
Sudden one afternoon, wrathful and dumb
And swinging a length of cable. It wasn't fear

That defeated us. It was surprise
That it mattered so much what we'd done.
How could we know? He'd been one of us all our lives,
So close it was hard to see how he'd beat us
This once: he was already man enough to think he loved a
    woman.

So he came down on us sudden, boys,
All of us, and he gave us a taste of the hurt
We'd live to know another way: how love
Can be wrong and still be the only joy
That's real: how, when we come to it,

We stand amazed but take the blow, transfigured, idiot.

Sex Ed

BETSY SHOLL

. . . . . .

Well-dressed, demure, jammed into those
politely arranged desks, it's hard to be
serious, but we are. No one even parts lips
to acknowledge what used to drive us crazy
in the back seats of cars, what kept us up
half the night reliving the last slow dance,
girl on her toes, guy bent at the knees
to press in against her.

The instructors speak precisely about
the importance of our children knowing the facts,
so surely none of us in our high heels and
neck ties is going to admit how our first mistakes
have suddenly blossomed so tender and lovely
we've been forgiven a thousand times,
a thousand times forgiven and repeated ourselves.

But fingering the graffiti on this desk,
I remember being braille to you, being read
like a steamy novel, and how those lessons
stayed with us, practical as driver's ed, those hours
of simulation behind the wheel of a parked car.
The truth is I don't regret having studied with you
though I do feel inarticulate, like an athlete
asked to speak in a room of kids, who has nothing
to say except, "practice, practice."

Once our daughter watched the cat in heat
yowl and slither across the floor, and without
looking up asked, would that happen to her. Sometimes
it isn't shame that makes us speechless. It's not
regret that makes me linger at the curb watching
her toss back her yellow hair and yank open
the heavy doors to school.

Third Day of Spring

SUSAN MURRAY

. . . . . .

The window is open.
The smell of spring.
Like sweet grass
and barefoot running.

But we are all trapped in
the stillness of the classroom.

Why did this teacher
(Oh, he is such a tyrant!)
open the window?

We shall never learn now.
Our minds are distracted
expanding off
and out.

Directions for Resisting the SAT

RICHARD HAGUE

. . . . . .

Do not believe in October or May
or in any Saturday morning with pencils.
Do not observe the rules of gravity,
commas, history.
Lie about numbers.
Blame your successes,
every one of them,
on rotten luck.
Resign all clubs and committees.
Go down with the ship—any ship.
Speak nothing like English.
Desire to live whole,
like an oyster or snail,
and follow no directions.
Listen to no one.

Make your marks on everything.

The Truant Officer's Helper

DAVID WAGONER

. . . . . .

My only day in the black
Old truant officer's truck,
Grandfather and I
Went lurching and jouncing
Over raw country roads
To find boys playing hooky.
Their mothers on sagging porches
With steel-gray hair coming down
The sides of their sad faces
Would say they didn't know
What their boys were up to
Or where in the world they were,
But my grandfather knew.

His voice as calm and soft
And sure as during grace,
He told their mothers on them:
They were fishing in Sippo Creek
Or fighting in alleys
Or playing with guinea pigs
In back of the hospital
Or sniping butts in gutters
Or swimming and taking leaks
In the town's pure drinking water,
Not listening to their teachers,
Not learning their three Rs.

Bad boys stayed out of school
With no excuse from doctors
Or mothers, dentists or fathers.
We hunted them everywhere:
In orchards and vacant lots,
In carbarns and pool halls
And down by the canal

Where bums held their own classes,
All those tempting places
I might have gone myself
If I'd been old
Or bad or brave enough.

By afternoon we'd caught
Only one guilty sinner
Red-handed with swiped berries,
Red hair still wet,
A trespassing skinny-dipper
From out at the gravel pit,
And we brought him back alive
To Henry Wadsworth Longfellow
Junior High School, hanging
His head. Grandfather told him
Never to yield to temptation,
Never to steal or tell stories,
To grow up good and smart
As a Presbyterian,
Then sent him to his Doom.

My mother knew where *I* was
And gave me a good excuse:
I was helping my grandfather
Find bad boys and refill
The shelves of a magic storehouse,
A cave of Ali Baba,
With jars of paste and notebooks
And chalk and bottles of ink
And rubber stamps and rulers.
Longfellow over the door
Told us the thoughts of youth
Were long, long thoughts, but mine
In that dim supply room
Were short as my light fingers.

That night in a shed loft
I flew with a featherbed

By lamplight, writing my first
Short story full of lies
About a secret country
And a boy who disobeyed
And ran away in a dream.
I tried hard to be good
And smart and made it up
Out of my own head
On that stolen paper,
My stolen pencil trembling.

God's Stopwatch

JIM DANIELS

. . . . . .

Kevin Hillman asked Sister Agatha
in seventh-grade science
how sperm got to the egg.
She blushed. *They swim,*
she said.

I said to Patty Flaherty
my sperms want to go swimming
with your eggs. I thought only
of Patty's polka-dotted panties.
She raised her skirt.
Oh, what alliteration!

*

The nuns were losing their habits
though the older ones hung on,
beating us with their black rosary beads.

I'm married to God, Sister Agatha
told us, wore a ring out in public —
without my habit on, men can't tell.
We snickered — her green dress
looked like the library curtains.

*

Patty's friend Lynn met up
with a strong swimmer that spring
and disappeared, only to return
the next fall looking the same,
only quieter.

At first she walked home alone
after school. It was like
she died. But we came back to her—
she was one of us, the opposite
of immaculate.

*

Larry Walton's little brother collapsed
and died on the playground. Bad heart.
Larry started stuttering. We gave him
the ball more often.

What could we do? Father Davis
talked to us about death.
What did he know, he was alive.

*

Father Davis talked to the boys
about sex. What did he know?

He told us don't do it.
Don't do it alone.
Don't do it with a girl.

The clock circled lazily.
He pulled at his collar.

*

When I held Patty's sweaty hand
an invisible host melted between us.

We never swam together, together
like that. It was enough then
to get beneath each other's habits
and see what was there
and touch what was there

so we could be true believers.

＊

Lynn's invisible baby replaced
Larry's brother. Somehow.
It was all we could figure.
We tried to create our own math
but it didn't work.

＊

In second grade, we liked the nun
who gave out candy. In fourth,
we liked the one who sang sweetly,
laughed sweetly.

In sixth we learned faith meant
if you asked *why* too many times,
they hit you.

＊

We swallowed the white hosts,
tasteless in our dry mouths.
We wanted moist color, tongue
on tongue.

Sister Agatha told us kissing
passionately for more than five seconds
was a sin. At lunch that day,
Patty and I headed straight to the closet
and started counting.

Field Trip to My First Time

JAMES HARMS

. . . . . .

No one called from the foot of the stairs.
But there we were anyway, showered
and snug in a fresh pair of jeans,

the table arrayed with toast
and two flavors of jelly;
it was difficult leaving the house.

The bus driver waited at the corner, engine idling
like a kitten in his lap, and everyone smiled
as we boarded. . . .

And in the end
we couldn't have known:
the brown grass for miles, like a sea

grown tired of rising into the sky,
of falling in pieces
so far from home,

the live oaks and lupine,
the dust, the picnic benches
crowded into the shade,

the other children and their same brown sacks,
three kinds of soda in a chest
by the bus.

And then the walk to the falls,
the three forbidden pools, a man
in a round hat, his skin as brown

as a belt, yelling above
the roar, explaining the story of snow
and spring, the long fall

to the bay, which we could "see in the distance,"
though none of us could, the smog
as thick as a filthy sweater.

Then Helen asked about Manuel,
whose sweatshirt hung from a yucca tree
at the foot of Falls Trail.

Someone yelled, "Search party!"
but Mrs. Ingalls insisted we sit.
And the man like a belt

left his hat with Bill Norton,
who wouldn't wear it, just balanced it
on his knees like a plate of hot food.

We tried to sing "Michael Row Your Boat"
but Mrs. Ingalls hissed.
"What about Twenty Questions?" suggested Sally Lee.

And so we waited without worry for the man
to return with Manuel, who fell
without a sound

from just below the top,
mixed in with the swirling water
and slid from one pool to the next,

then floated by us like a clump of old sticks;
we almost didn't notice him. I'd never seen
someone dead. It was my first time.

Field Trip to the Mill

PATRICIA DOBLER

. . . . . .

Sister Monica has her hands full
timing the climb to the catwalk
so the fourth-graders are lined up
before the next heat is tapped, "and no
giggling no jostling, you monkeys!
So close to the edge!" She passes out
sourballs for bribes, not liking
the smile on the foreman's face,
the way he pulls at his cap,
he's not Catholic. Protestant madness,
these field trips, this hanging from catwalks
suspended over an open hearth.

Sister Monica understands Hell
to be like this. If overhead cranes clawing
their way through layers of dark air
grew leathery wings and flew screeching
at them, it wouldn't surprise her.
And the three warning whistle blasts,
the blazing orange heat pouring out
liquid fire like Devil's soup
doesn't surprise her. She understands
Industry and Capital and Labor,
the Protestant trinity. That is why
she trembles here, the children clinging
to her as she watches them learn their future.

5 / Sports and Clubs

First Grade

WILLIAM STAFFORD

. . . . . .

In the play Amy didn't want to be
anybody; so she managed the curtain.
Sharon wanted to be Amy. But Sam
wouldn't let anybody be anybody else —
he said it was wrong. "All right," Steve said,
"I'll be me, but I don't like it."
So Amy was Amy, and we didn't have the play.
And Sharon cried.

The High School Band

REED WHITTEMORE

. . . . . .

On warm days in September the high school band
Is up with the birds and marches along our street,
Boom, boom,
To a field where it goes boom boom until eight forty-five
When it marches, as in the old rhyme, back, boom boom,
To its study halls, leaving our street
Empty except for the leaves that descend to no drum,
And lie still.
In September
A great many high school bands beat a great many drums,
And the silences after their partings are very deep.

First Practice

GARY GILDNER

. . . . . .

After the doctor checked to see
we weren't ruptured,
the man with the short cigar took us
under the grade school,
where we went in case of attack
or storm, and said
he was Clifford Hill, he was
a man who believed dogs
ate dogs, he had once killed
for his country, and if
there were any girls present
for them to leave now.

                        No one
left. OK, he said, he said I take
that to mean you are hungry
men who hate to lose as much
as I do. OK. Then
he made two lines of us
facing each other,
and across the way, he said,
is the man you hate most
in the world,
and if we are to win
that title I want to see how.
But I don't want to see
any marks when you're dressed,
he said. He said, *Now*.

Homecoming

DORIANNE LAUX

. . . . . .

At the high school football game, the boys
stroke their new muscles, the girls sweeten their lips
with gloss that smells of bubblegum, candy cane,
or cinnamon. In pleated cheerleader skirts
they walk home with each other, practicing yells,
their long bare legs forming in the dark.
Under the arched field lights a girl
in a velvet prom dress stands near the chainlink,
a cone of roses held between her breasts.
Her lanky father, in a corduroy suit, leans
against the fence. While they talk, she slips a foot
in and out of a new white pump, fingers the weave
of her French braid, the glittering earrings.
They could be a couple on their first date, she,
a little shy, he, trying to impress her
with his casual stance. This is the moment
when she learns what she will love: a warm night,
the feel of nylon between her thighs, the fine hairs
on her arms lifting when a breeze
sifts in through the bleachers, cars
igniting their engines, a man bending over her,
smelling the flowers pressed against her neck.

For the Cheerleaders of Garfield High

COLLEEN J. MCELROY

. . . . . .

In pom-poms and perfume
They're picture perfect
Palm wine drinkers scream
As they spin and leap
Each motion set
For stop action
A flash of blackberry thigh
An arched neck
Lifting a satin chin
Then bursts of light
As they collapse
Giggling in rhyme
They take you back
To any hometown game
Backs like graceful strings
On a harp blend
And flow with their arms
Making music in space
Catching strains of the Sahara
They weave a cat's cradle
Of dreams, these girls
Who could wash rice
On a mud floor
Wearing mink.

Autumn Begins in Martins Ferry, Ohio

JAMES WRIGHT

. . . . . .

In the Shreve High football stadium,
I think of Polacks nursing long beers in Tiltonsville,
And gray faces of Negroes in the blast furnace at Benwood,
And the ruptured night watchman of Wheeling Steel,
Dreaming of heroes.

All the proud fathers are ashamed to go home.
Their women cluck like starved pullets,
Dying for love.

Therefore,
Their sons grow suicidally beautiful
At the beginning of October,
And gallop terribly against each other's bodies.

At Navajo Monument Valley Tribal School

SHERMAN ALEXIE

. . . . . .

from the photograph by Skeet McAuley

the football field rises
to meet the mesa. Indian boys
gallop across the grass, against

the beginning of their body.
On those Saturday afternoons,
unbroken horses gather to watch

their sons growing larger
in the small parts of the world.
Everyone is the quarterback.

There is no thin man in a big hat
writing down all the names
in two columns: winners and losers.

This is the eternal football game,
Indians versus Indians. All the Skins
in the wooden bleachers, fancydancing,

stomping red dust straight down
into nothing. Before the game is over,
the eighth-grade girls' track team

comes running, circling the field,
their thin and brown legs echoing
wild horses, wild horses, wild horses.

Hockey Season

ROBIN BECKER

. . . . . .

Maples, willows, sycamores hid the field
behind the Lower School & meeting house.
We ran in light blue tunics billowing
like maternity tops, cloth sashes looped
round our necks. Elastic from the bloomers
left little marks circling our thighs.
New limestone lines streaked the grass.
                              Annie charged
towards the goal; in a year she'd be at Radcliffe,
later in Switzerland studying tree rings.
Past the halfback from Stevens School,
past their fullbacks, both teams
on her tail, she lifted the ball over to Megan
                              who flicked it in.
I jogged in the wings, my stick in my hands.
Their goalie tightened her knee pads;
everyone was hugging & jumping up & down;
I heard cheers from the stands; I had half the field
to myself & pictured Corky Miller, who, senior year,
led the team to a winning season,
her grown-up thighs pumping past the players.
She wore the plaid tunic of the varsity squad,
& when I met her on the stairs,
                              I had nothing to say.
I recall the smell of the oranges
the mothers served at half time,
the way we sat in a circle talking about the plays,
the stickiness of the lumpy wax we passed around
to preserve the wood on the snub-nosed sticks.
The light faded; we crowded into the cars,
exhausted, clutching our Latin books,
pressed against one another
in the cold November air.

The Pageant

MICHAEL COLLIER

. . . . . .

When Brian McCarthy, the male lead
in our third-grade, Spanish-class
production of *Alice in Wonderland*,

didn't show, Mrs. Carrera's husband,
Tito, had to read lines from the wings,
where he also managed the plywood

and canvas scenery. Paunchy, in a white
T-shirt, sleeves covering tattooed anchors,
he lost whole sentences in drapery

and screens, which made Alice, the precocious
Diane Grasso, bossier than ever, more confident,
so that she served up tildes and rolled

r's like virtuoso yo-yo tricks.
The pageant made city news in the morning paper:
a photograph framed by the ratty proscenium

of the social hall, in which Mrs. Carrera
occupies the foreground, holding
her blue-and-red velveteen

needlepoint portrait of Kennedy
(her scapular of gratitude for America)
while the cast stands by height

in tiers behind her, and Tito out of sight
in the wings smokes in his folding chair,
a hand on the drapery cords, his feet

propped on the tiny canvas door he made
for Alice.

In the Elementary School Choir

GREGORY DJANIKIAN

. . . . . .

I had never seen a cornfield in my life,
I had never been to Oklahoma,
But I was singing as loud as anyone,
"Oh what a beautiful morning. . . . The corn
Is as high as an elephant's eye,"
Though I knew something about elephants I thought,
Coming from the same continent as they did,
And they being more like camels than anything else.

And when we sang from *Meet Me in St. Louis,*
"Clang, clang, clang went the trolley,"
I remembered the ride from Ramleh Station
In the heart of Alexandria
All the way to Roushdy where my grandmother lived,
The autos on the roadway vying
With mule carts and bicycles,
The Mediterranean half a mile off on the left,
The air smelling sharply of diesel and salt.

It was a problem which had dogged me
For a few years, this confusion of places,
And when in 5th grade geography I had pronounced
"Des Moines" as though it were a village in France,
Mr. Kephart led me to the map on the front wall,
And so I'd know where I was,
Pressed my forehead squarely against Iowa.
Des Moines, he'd said. Rhymes with coins.

Now we were singing "zippidy-doo-dah, zippidy-ay,"
And every song we'd sung had in it
Either sun or bluebirds, fair weather
Or fancy fringe, O beautiful America!
And one tier below me,
There was Linda Deemer with her amber waves

And lovely fruited plains,
And she was part of America too
Along with sun and spacious sky
Though untouchable, and as distant
As purple mountains of majesty.

"This is my country," we sang,
And a few years ago there would have been
A scent of figs in the air, mangoes,
And someone playing the oud along a clear stream.

But now it was "My country 'tis of thee"
And I sang it out with all my heart
And now with Linda Deemer in mind.
"Land where my fathers died," I bellowed,
And it was not too hard to imagine
A host of my great uncles and grandfathers
Stunned from their graves in the Turkish interior
And finding themselves suddenly
On a rock among maize and poultry
And Squanto shaking their hands.

How could anyone not think America
was exotic when it had Massachusetts
And the long tables of thanksgiving?
And how could it not be home
If it were the place where love first struck?

We had finished singing.
The sun was shining through large windows
On the beatified faces of all
Who had sung well and with feeling.
We were ready to file out and march back
To our room where Mr. Kephart was waiting.
Already Linda Deemer had disappeared
Into the high society of the hallway.
One day I was going to tell her something.
Des Moines, I was saying to myself,
Baton Rouge. Terre Haute. Boise.

Junior High Dance

ALLISON JOSEPH

. . . . . .

No one wanted to dance with us
in 8th grade, to glide across
the shiny expanse of gym floor,
choosing us from among
the awkward and shy girls,
the boys loud and pushing instead,
uncouth to everyone but chaperones.
I had on the ugliest pantsuit—
matching orange and blue—
homemade by my mother before
she really learned to sew,
before she dazzled us with
cotton and corduroy.
My best friend had an earache,
but stayed anyway, swaying
to the music, letting it
carry her heavy body
a little forward, away
from the wall, back.
The speakers didn't wail
the way I wanted them to,
their volume respectable,
although you could still hear
Diana Ross singing—*I'm coming out*—
her anthem of disco liberation.
We watched the other kids dance,
lithe Hispanic girls who always
seemed to know when to turn,
how to bow and shimmy, or smile.
Watched the older black girls
who, self-satisfied and worldly wise,
knew all the latest steps,
and the variations on the latest
steps, so when I dared once before

to venture on the dance floor,
they hooted at me, said *that's old*,
with surety they had about nothing
else. April and I hung back,
sassy wallflowers joking about
our teachers—their whiteness,
their lack of street savvy.
They still thought Diana Ross
was a Supreme, that she still sang
You Can't Hurry Love with Flo and Mary,
that Motown was still Hitsville, U.S.A.
No one could convince us
we had something to learn
from them, no one could tell us
they were anything more than old
as they blew up balloons,
made sure the lights stayed on.
And we had our corner,
our tiny bit of that place,
where we listened to that garish
seventies music, not letting
our bodies stray far, staying
right there, no matter how funky
the beat, no matter how delicious.

Going Full-Court

JOHN REPP

. . . . . .

Johnnie Redfern would rise above
Big Steve and dunk or fade away,
his weightless ease transfixing us
despite our need to burn him

and the other blacks we went
full-court with on Sundays
in the park our folks said
we'd never survive till the city

cleaned it up. What bodies we had
at seventeen, how true
my shot from the baseline
and what glee to hit it

over Johnnie. Strange, I recall
his lashes and thin eyebrows
most clearly. How little I knew him
or could have, though

once or twice we talked music
or maybe girls, I don't know,
but I remember wanting to say
how much I liked his moves

and the way he pissed off Big Steve
by taking all the elbows
and scoring at will, with both hands.
Basketball became the least of things

that spring, once the black kids
shut the high school down. I sat
on the heater in homeroom, watching
for my father's car, not knowing

how he'd get through the crowds,
not knowing a gang of whites
would be jumping blacks tomorrow,
or that I could open the yearbook

thirty years later and point
to the cop with his nightstick raised,
to Michelle Brown looking back at him,
her feet poised over the tar.

The School

DAVID HUDDLE

. . . . . .

On one side the high school, on the other
grades one through seven, the purple-curtained
auditorium shrank and grew shabbier
each August we came back. Mr. Whitt one year
decided Charles Tomlinson, Slick King, Dwayne
Burchett, Bobby Peaks, and Big Face Cather
could be a basketball team. They practiced
on a rocky, red-dirt court with a basket
and some boards on a post. They drove to games
—always at the other school—in Slick's Ford.
Uniforms were jeans and T-shirts. Big Face
and Bobby played barefoot. They lost by scores
like ten to ninety-three, unaccustomed to such space,
wooden floors, lights, adults calling them names.

Cheerleaders

LISA COFFMAN

. . . . . .

Out of the American provinces
regarded by many as exile
one is born into—
evolves the oddity of a girl
to whom her own opinions pose a danger
yet able to shout, pinioned
in the execution of a complex-figured leap
before any number of audience, local, or from nearby towns.

Admitting "their attitude is like that of strippers,"
admit a scrubbed citric innocence to the sex.
No Venus grins here from the foam, curl ends tweaked water-
　　dark:
the hair fanned across the inwardly groaning boy's fourth-period
　　desk
has been ironed flat or flipped up,
the hairless lotioned calves end in sock folds,
the chest is topped demurely with a carpet letter.

As for the bruited away-bus escapades of sex:
these are more often exaggerations
in the nature of all town troubadours.
The intent is, rather, "to be kissproof:
put on lipstick, then have someone
powder your lips through a piece of tissue. Do
not inhale." Not admired by majestic-thighed women
passing in and out of steamroom steam
are the somnolent voices roused to staccato, single drawn word
　　starting
low ending loud, childish bell still to go *OH* go *OH*
as the lead girl takes her hands from her hips
among all eight waiting in identical postures
and puts the bunny-ear shape of her sneaker to an in-place
　　prancing

or strikes the wooden court boards hard
until the stands start ringing back.

Even admitting the ingenuity of their pleats
that allow the skirt to extend straight from the waist,
and the athletic rigor required for certain jumps,
no one accuses cheerleaders of usefulness:
they are discarded at the end of high schools
excluded from cabinet meetings and businesses,

yet, while it is known
"there are no women like that, anywhere!"
as the young photographer cried, home
from retouching hair and blemishes
on women already exemplary for beauty,

his girlfriend and sisters in the magazine-
littered living room
merely looked at him, then went on with their reading.

When Your Father Is Also
Your Wrestling Coach

ANDREW WILSON

. . . . . .

When your father is also your wrestling coach,
you are acquainted with the winter-white skin of
his legs, and with the knife-lines of his knees:
whiter than white, and like the c-glyphs of calculus.

Expressing the perfect form of a single-leg takedown,
you wrap your arms around that whiteness—your
father's thinning leg. Your face kisses his knee.
You suck his knee in tight against your chest and
it's your father there, bouncing, balancing on his
remaining leg. Your head becomes a lever,
pressing tired joints, working him to the mat.

Maintain a low center.
Eye toward the navel.
Back straight.
It is all as he taught you and
he wants you to bring him down, hard.

Your father who is also your wrestling coach
will make you see significance in seasons.
Young will murder old. The thought creeps
like something spilled, becomes as clear to you
as your father's balding crown. You study
that naked place as you break your father
down to his belly, begin to pin him.

You recall the bluish hue of his feet in the shower.
His feet were childish: lineless, translucent, with
so much bone. There was bone everywhere and
his testicles drooped toward the earth like book bags.

He lets you pin him, but you know there has been no
Great Mutation, not yet. His chin tilts upward; his eyes
speak the language of men, and you are bound to listen.
Under the gathered skin of his arms, sinews twist like wire.
His biceps still dance, are nimble, are potent as dogs.

Therefore, when your father is also your wrestling coach
you learn shame. Losses are recorded not in tears but in
the way you hate to see your father sit there afterward,
softly speaking with men. "He cannot tell them I won,"
you think. "He would like to."

I wish you a winning season.
Wrestle your match.
Don't muscle your man.
There is a gentleness about wrestling, rarely comprehended.
Master that, then move with explosion, slicker than slick.
It is all as your father taught you.

Look, and there's your father in your corner,
legs planted, hands cupped around mouth, directing.
Vie, clash in the light of his straight stare;
know that it's you he sees there.

Passing

JIM DANIELS

. . . . . .

In gym class boxing, Fat Feeney got paired
with Big Eddie Lavendar. Coach Wendler
circled the ring, taunted Feeney,
pushed him back when he tried to run.

Lavendar flattened Feeney's nose.
He wouldn't get up. Lay there frozen,
an iceberg waiting for arctic silence.
We filed past to the locker room
kicking him, spitting out all our names
for boys like him who wouldn't fight.

   *

The High Dive: *A* for a dive. *C* for a jump.
F for sissies. Feeney climbed up, jiggling
layers of flesh. We wanted to see the splash.
Coach screamed *Jump Feeney jump*!
We chanted *Jump Feeney jump*!
Our voices echoed off tile, rang out
over still water. Feeney held the rail.
His tears fell to the board. We waited, screaming,
bare-assed on the benches.
When he climbed down, Wendler paddled him.
In the locker room, our arms popped out,
punched him between the rows.

   *

Doug Molinski stomped on Feeney's face
in the parking lot. Everyone knew
he never fought back, a punching bag
for anyone's random black-and-blue anger.

Molinski wouldn't stop because,
because, who knows. Feeney's face
a bloody mess surgery couldn't fix.

Coach used to yell
You're a big boy, Feeney,
hit somebody, as if those two things
went hand in hand. Molinski back in a year.
Feeney's mother took him away—who knows where.
You know how dogs can sniff out fear?
Yeah, I punched him a few times:
jab, jab, jab. I took my *C.*

Instruction

CONRAD HILBERRY

. . . . . .

The coach has taught her how to swing,
run bases, slide, how to throw
to second, flip off her mask for fouls.

Now, on her own, she studies
how to knock the dirt out of her cleats,
hitch up her pants, miss her shoulder
with a stream of spit, bump
her fist into her catcher's mitt,
and stare incredulously at the ump.

Stuart Rieger

MEL GLENN

. . . . . .

Inscriptions in my yearbook:
"Best Wishes," (eight of them).
"Good Luck," (six of them).
"Keep in Touch," (four of them).
"Have a Nice Life," (two of them).
Wonderful!
Surely, four years could have produced more,
A little more feeling, a lot more warmth.
But the fault is mine, fellow graduates.
When you went to football games, parties, and dances,
I stayed home and studied my brains out,
Always worried that this quiz or that test
Would irrevocably determine my future.
I made my choice to live in the future tense
And forfeited all happiness in the present one.
So, forgive me if I just sign your book, "Best Wishes."
It's the best I can do under the circumstances.

6 / After school

The Supremes

CORNELIUS EADY

. . . . . .

We were born to be gray. We went to school,
Sat in rows, ate white bread,
Looked at the floor a lot. In the back
Of our small heads

A long scream. We did what we could,
And all we could do was
Turn on each other. How the fat kids suffered!
Not even being jolly could save them.

And then there were the anal retentives,
The terrified brown-noses, the desperately
Athletic or popular. This, of course,
Was training. At home

Our parents shook their heads and waited.
We learned of the industrial revolution,
The sectioning of the clock into pie slices.
We drank cokes and twiddled our thumbs. In the
Back of our minds

A long scream. We snapped butts in the showers,
Froze out shy girls on the dance floor,
Pin-pointed flaws like radar.
Slowly we understood: this was to be the world.

We were born insurance salesmen and secretaries,
Housewives and short order cooks,
Stock room boys and repairmen,
And it wouldn't be a bad life, they promised,
In a tone of voice that would force some of us
To reach in self-defense for wigs,
Lipstick,

Sequins.

Recess

COLLEEN J. MCELROY

. . . . . .

I come here alone   standing wet
and poetic in the rain
the school is still the same
dusty windows reflect dogs
stuck inside a chain link fence
bricks smoothed by a thousand
tennis shoes and slamming doors
dull glass squares hide
rooms full of radiator smells
windows like checkered eyes
defying truants
in Sioux City, Biloxi, and St. Louis
I watch from the playground
and play out memories
each ghost a marble in my game
my new suede boots sound hollow
clumsy on these quick stones
I haunt friends

ten of us run blindly for a swing
kick a loose ball rolling by a line
of second graders   we're older, wise
even wiser now there's only six
four of us died
comics in a war for Captain Kidd
the rest prayed
stood in front of open graves
in wispy groups
like in the fifth
where we warbled long division
that the veins of my hands remember
when I lift a wine glass
to toast Virginia's last baby
her tenth   he lays too quiet in the crib

she stands as before
head leaning slightly to the side
at ten that pose would hide
pigtails as she stood at the board
wandering through prose rules
for saying things just so
she married Harry
always falling off his seat
smelled of unwashed socks
still does   smelled even worse
when he was shot by a cop

it's all there under the chalk dust
the Elmer's glue   x sum squared
and sandwiches stuck to wax paper
today's big dealer
sits between another war's hero
and a mother of ten
he picks his nose   she watches
the rain fall in wet strings
out there where I stand
wet   smoking   thinking poet
thinking   smoking in the rain

What Saves Us

BRUCE WEIGL

. . . . . .

We are wrapped around each other
in the back of my father's car parked
in the empty lot of the high school
of our failures, sweat on her neck
like oil. The next morning I would leave
for the war and I thought I had something
coming for that, I thought to myself
that I would not die never having
been inside her body. I lifted
her skirt above her waist like an umbrella
blown inside out by the storm. I pulled
her cotton panties up as high
as she could stand. I was on fire. Heaven
was in sight. We were drowning
on our tongues and I tried
to tear my pants off when she stopped
so suddenly we were surrounded
only by my shuddering
and by the school bells
grinding in the empty halls.
She reached to find something,
a silver crucifix on a silver chain,
the tiny savior's head
hanging, and stakes through his hands and his feet.
She put it around my neck and held me
so long my heart's black wings were calmed.
We are not always right
about what we think will save us.
I thought that dragging the angel down that night
would save me, but I carried the crucifix in my pocket
and rubbed it on my face and lips
nights the rockets roared in.
People die sometimes so near you,
you feel them struggling to cross over,
the deep untangling, of one body from another.

Class Reunion

ANN DARR

Ring the old school bell,
we are coming home. We cluster
together only a little.
The chance that brought us
into one class was passion
or duty. Born within
the six necessary months,
we were fifteen small colts
to be broken or led to
water and books.

Three can't come back:
one was killed in a war,
one was mashed at the wheel of her car,
one sickened and died of
complications.
The rest of us have died a little.
Could I come out of curiosity?

Correction: our soldier is already there.
The government said yes
so he came home by boat in a box.
(Madame President of
the Alumni Society: It won't
interest you to know
that I speak with him often.
I don't know why, but he turns up in dreams
more often than I can account for.
It won't interest you because
I won't tell you. Because
then you would know I am as mad
as you always knew I was.)

Dear Belle:
I am so sorry. Any
other day but May nineteenth.
I have not seen you all for twenty years.
With God's help I shall escape for still
another twenty.
Love,
if you can,
Ann.

Now I will take a red pencil
and re-vein my heart.

Marcus Millsap

School Day Afternoon

DAVE ETTER

. . . . . .

I climb the steps of the yellow school bus,
move to a seat in back, and we're off,
bouncing along the bumpy blacktop.
What am I going to do when I get home?
I'm going to make myself a sugar sandwich
and go outdoors and look at the birds
and the gigantic blue silo
they put up across the road at Motts'.
This weekend we're going to the farm show.
I like roosters and pigs, but farming's no fun.
When I get old enough to do something big,
I'd like to grow orange trees in a greenhouse.
Or maybe I'll drive a school bus
and yell at the kids when I feel mad:
"Shut up back there, you hear me?"
At last, my house, and I grab my science book
and hurry down the steps into the sun.
There's Mr. Mott, staring at his tractor.
He's wearing his DeKalb cap
with the crazy winged ear of corn on it.
He wouldn't wave over here to me
if I was handing out hundred dollar bills.
I'll put brown sugar on my bread this time,
then go lie around by the water pump,
where the grass is very green and soft,
soft as the body of a red-winged blackbird.
Imagine, a blue silo to stare at,
and Mother not coming home till dark!

Flash Cards

RITA DOVE

. . . . . .

In math I was the whiz kid, keeper
of oranges and apples. *What you don't understand,
master*, my father said; the faster
I answered, the faster they came.

I could see one bud on the teacher's geranium,
one clear bee sputtering at the wet pane.
The tulip trees always dragged after heavy rain
so I tucked my head as my boots slapped home.

My father put up his feet after work
and relaxed with a highball and *The Life of Lincoln*.
After supper we drilled and I climbed the dark

before sleep, before a thin voice hissed
numbers as I spun on a wheel. I had to guess.
Ten, I kept saying, *I'm only ten*.

Pass/Fail

LINDA PASTAN

. . . . . .

Examination dreams are reported to persist even into old age . . .
—Time *magazine*

You will never graduate
from this dream
of blue books.
No matter how
you succeed awake,
asleep there is a test
waiting to be failed.
The dream beckons
with two dull pencils,
but you haven't even
taken the course;
when you reach for a book—
it closes its door
in your face; when
you conjugate a verb—
it is in the wrong
language.
Now the pillow becomes
a blank page. Turn it
to the cool side;
you will still smother
in all of the feathers
that have to be learned
by heart.

M. Degas Teaches Art & Science at Durfee Intermediate School

PHILIP LEVINE

. . . . . .

Detroit, 1942

He made a line on the blackboard,
one bold stroke from right to left
diagonally downward and stood back
to ask, looking as always at no one
in particular, "What have I done?"
From the back of the room Freddie
shouted, "You've broken a piece
of chalk." M. Degas did not smile.
"What have I done?" he repeated.
The most intellectual students
looked down to study their desks
except for Gertrude Bimmler, who raised
her hand before she spoke. "M. Degas,
you have created the hypotenuse
of an isosceles triangle." Degas mused.
Everyone knew that Gertrude could not
be incorrect. "It is possible,"
Louis Warshowsky added precisely,
"that you have begun to represent
the roof of a barn." I remember
that it was exactly twenty minutes
past eleven, and I thought at worst
this would go on another forty
minutes. It was early April,
the snow had all but melted on
the playgrounds, the elms and maples
bordering the cracked walks shivered
in the new winds, and I believed
that before I knew it I'd be
swaggering to the candy store
for a Milky Way. M. Degas

pursed his lips, and the room
stilled until the long hand
of the clock moved to twenty one
as though in complicity with Gertrude,
who added confidently, "You've begun
to separate the dark from the dark."
I looked back for help, but now
the trees bucked and quaked, and I
knew this could go on forever.

Bonfire

PAUL B. JANECZKO

. . . . . .

That summer
school ended
with a half-day Tuesday.
But before baseball
　　fishing
　　　　reading comics
　　　　　　tenting out
we carried notebooks, tests, and compositions
to a cleared spot
at the edge of the ball field
and began the tearing and crumpling of pages:
the quiz we took the morning
Mrs. Hamilton backed her black Buick
over her trash cans;
the report on flax I delivered
the day of the hurricane,
when a wedge of the ceiling collapsed
on the Blessed Virgin
and we prayed;
the composition Raymond wrote
the day he wore his mother's blonde wig to school;
teeth-marked yellow pencils—
mostly no. 2s with flat erasers;
and penmanship workbooks
filled with the proper swirls and curls.
Even holy cards
of robed smileless saints
and lists of spelling demons
were ready to burn.

One wooden match
struck on my belt buckle
was enough
to start the flames
that let
eighth grade dance
away.

Dropout

WILLIAM STAFFORD

. . . . . .

Grundy and Hoagland and all the rest who ganged
our class and wrecked the high school gym for fun —
you thought of them last night, and how they laughed
when they beat up a Mexican.

Later they marched against Hitler youth, but admired
them too — how they were brave and sang: "Why,
you should see how those troops fought!" And Hoagland
came home to a job with the FBI.

Remember the team? — the celebration in the Lions
Hall? — with Coach Gist there, a real man? —
the speeches? — the jackrabbit chile? You looked through the smoke
and the smokey jokes, and vomited.

And never went back again.

Graduation Notes

for Mungu, Morani, Monica and
Andrew and Crefield Seniors

SONIA SANCHEZ

. . . . . .

So much of growing up is an unbearable waiting. A constant
longing for another time. Another season.

I remember walking like you today down this path. In love with
the day. Flesh awkward. I sang at the edge of adolescence and the
scent of adulthood rushed me and I thought I would suffocate. But
I didn't. I am here. So are you. Finally. Tired of tiny noises your
eyes hum a large vibration.

I think all journeys are the same. My breath delighting in the
single dawn. Yours. Walking at the edge. Unafraid. Anxious for the
unseen dawns are mixing today like the underground rhythms
seeping from your pores.

At this moment your skins living your eighteen years suspend
all noises. Your days still half-opened, crackle like the fires to come.
Outside. The earth. Wind. Night. Unfold for you. Listen to their
sounds. They have sung me seasons that never abandoned me. A
dance of summer rain. A ceremony of thunder waking up the earth
to human monuments.

Facing each other I smile at your faces. Know you as young
heroes soon to be decorated with years. Hope no wars dwarf you.
Know your dreams wild and sweet will sail from your waists to
surround the non-lovers. Dreamers. And you will rise up like
newborn armies refashioning lives. Louder than the sea you
come from.

Uncle Seagram

GWENDOLYN BROOKS

. . . . . .

My uncle likes me too much.

I am five and a half years old, and in kindergarten.
In kindergarten everything is clean.

My uncle is six feet tall with seven bumps on his chin.
My uncle is six feet tall, and he stumbles.
He stumbles because of his Wonderful Medicine
packed in his pocket all times.

Family is ma and pa and my uncle,
three brothers, three sisters, and me.

Every night at my house we play checkers and dominoes.
My uncle sits *close*.
There aren't any shoes or socks on his feet.
Under the table a big toe tickles my ankle.
Under the oilcloth his thin knee beats into mine.
And mashes. And mashes.

When we look at TV
my uncle picks *me* to sit on his lap.
As I sit, he gets hard in the middle.
I squirm, but he keeps me, and kisses my ear.

I am not even a girl.

Once, when I went to the bathroom,
my uncle noticed, came in, shut the door,
put his long white tongue in my ear,
and whispered "We're Best Friends, and Family,
and we know how to keep Secrets."

My uncle likes me too much. I am worried.

I do not like my uncle anymore.

David Talamántez on the Last
Day of Second Grade

ROSEMARY CATACALOS

. . . . . .

San Antonio, Texas, 1988

David Talamántez, whose mother is at work, leaves his mark
    everywhere in the schoolyard,
tosses pages from a thick sheaf of lined paper high in the air one
    by one, watches them

catch on the teachers' car bumpers, drift into the chalky narrow
    shade of the water fountain.
One last batch, stapled together, he rolls tight into a makeshift
    horn through which he shouts

David! and *David, yes!* before hurling it away hard and darting
    across Brazos Street against
the light, the little sag of head and shoulders when, safe on the
    other side, he kicks a can

in the gutter and wanders toward home. David Talamántez
    believes birds are warm blooded,
the way they are quick in the air and give out long strings of
    complicated music, different

all the time, not like cats and dogs. For this he was marked down
    in Science, and for putting
his name in the wrong place, on the right with the date instead
    on the left with Science

Questions, and for not skipping a line between his heading and
    answers. The X's for wrong
things are big, much bigger than David Talamántez's tiny writing.
    Write larger, his teacher says

in red ink across the tops of many pages. *Messy!* she says on
    others where he's erased
and started over, erased and started over. Spelling, Language
    Expression, Sentences Using

the Following Words. *Neck. I have a neck name. No!* 20's, 30's.
    Think again! He's good
in Art, though, makes 70 on Reading Station Artist's Corner,
    where he's traced and colored

an illustration from *Henny Penny.* A goose with red-and-white
    striped shirt, a hen in a turquoise
dress. Points off for the birds, cloud and butterfly he's drawn in
    freehand. *Not in the original*

picture! Twenty-five points off for writing nothing in the blank
    after *This is my favorite scene*
in the book because. . . . There's a page called Rules. *Listen!*
    Always working! Stay in your seat!

Raise your hand before you speak! No fighting! Be quiet! Rules
    copied from the board, no grade,
only a huge red checkmark. Later there is a test on Rules. *Listen!*
    Alay ercng! Sast in ao snet!

Rars aone bfo your spek! No finagn! Be cayt! He gets 70 on
    Rules, 10 on Spelling. An old man
stoops to pick up a crumpled drawing of a large family crowded
    around a table, an apartment

with bars on the windows in Alazán Courts, a huge sun in one
    corner saying, *To mush noys!*
After correcting the spelling, the grade is 90. *Nice details!* And
    there's another mark, on this paper

and all the others, the one in the doorway of La Rosa Beauty
   Shop, the one that blew under
the pool table at La Tenampa, the ones older kids have wadded
   up like big spit balls, the ones run

over by cars. On every single page David Talamántez has crossed
   out the teacher's red numbers
and written in giant letters, blue ink, *Yes! David, yes!*

7 / 0 Where Are They Now?

The Nuns of Childhood

Two Views

MAXINE KUMIN

. . . . . .

1

O where are they now, your harridan nuns
who thumped on young heads with a metal thimble
and punished with rulers your upturned palms:

three smacks for failing in long division,
one more to instill the meaning of *humble*.
As the twig is bent, said your harridan nuns.

Once, a visiting bishop, serene
at the close of a Mass through which he had shambled,
smiled upon you with upturned palms.

"Because this is my feast day," he ended,
"you may all have a free afternoon." In the scramble
of whistles and cheers one harridan nun,

fiercest of all the parochial coven,
Sister Pascala, without preamble
raged, "I protest!" and rapping on palms

at random, had bodily to be restrained.
O God's perfect servant is kneeling on brambles
wherever they sent her, your harridan nun,
enthroned as a symbol with upturned palms.

O where are they now, my darling nuns
whose heads were shaved under snowy wimples,
who rustled drily inside their gowns,

disciples of Oxydol, starch and bluing,
their backyard clothesline a pious example?
They have flapped out of sight, my darling nuns.

Seamless as fish, made all of one skin,
their language secret, these gentle vestals
were wedded to Christ inside their gowns.

O Mother Superior Rosarine
on whose lap the privileged visitor lolled
—I at age four with my darling nuns,

with Sister Elizabeth, Sister Ann,
am offered to Jesus, the Jewish child-
next-door, who worships your ample black gown,

your eyebrows, those thick mustachioed twins,
your rimless glasses, your ring of pale gold—
who can have stolen my darling nuns?
Who rustles drily inside my gown?

Shapes, Vanishings

HENRY TAYLOR

. . . . . .

1

Down a street in the town where I went
to high school twenty-odd years ago, by doorways
and shadows that change with the times, I walked
past a woman at whose glance I almost stopped cold,
almost to speak, to remind her of who I had been —
but walked on, not being certain it was she,
not knowing what I might find to say.
It wasn't quite the face I remembered, the years
being what they are, and I could have been wrong.

2

But that feeling of being stopped cold, stopped dead,
will not leave me, and I hark back
to the thing I remember her for, though God knows
how I could remind her of it now.
Well, one afternoon when I was fifteen
I sat in her class. She leaned on her desk,
facing us, the blackboard behind her arrayed
with geometrical figures — triangle, square,
pentagon, hexagon, *et cetera*. She pointed
and named them. "The five-sided figure," she said,
"is a polygon." So far so good, but then when she said
"The six-sided one is a hexagon," I wanted things clear.
Three or more sides is *poly*, I knew, but five only
is *penta*, and said so; she denied it,
and I pressed the issue, I, with no grades
to speak of, a miserable average to stand on
with an Archimedean pole — no world to move,
either, just a fact to get straight, but she
would have none of it, saying at last, "Are you
contradicting me?"

3

A small thing to remember a teacher for. Since then,
I have thought about justice often enough
to have earned my uncertainty about what it is,
but one hard fact from that day has stayed with me:
If you're going to be a smartass, you have to be right,
and not just some of the time. "Are you
contradicting me?" she had said, and I stopped
breathing a moment, the burden of her words
pressing down through me hard and quick, the huge
weight of knowing I was right, and beaten. She
had me. "No, ma'am," I managed to say, wishing
I had the whole thing down on tape to play back
to the principal, wishing I were ten feet tall
and never mistaken, ever, about anything in this world,
wishing I were older, and long gone from there.

4

Now I am older, and long gone from there.
What sense in a grudge over something so small?
What use to forgive her for something
she wouldn't remember? Now students
face me as I stand at my desk, and the shoe
may yet find its way to the other foot,
if it hasn't already. I couldn't charge
thirty-five cents for all that I know
of geometry; what little I learned is gone now,
like a face looming up for a second out of years
that dissolve in the mind like a single summer.
Therefore,
if ever she almost stops me again,
I will walk on as I have done once already,
remembering how we failed each other,
knowing better than to blame anyone.

Execution

EDWARD HIRSCH

· · · · · ·

The last time I saw my high school football coach
He had cancer stenciled into his face
Like pencil marks from the sun, like intricate
Drawings on the chalkboard, small *x*'s and *o*'s
That he copied down in a neat numerical hand
Before practice in the morning. By day's end
The board was a spiderweb of options and counters,
Blasts and sweeps, a constellation of players
Shining under his favorite word, *Execution*,
Underlined in the upper right-hand corner of things.
He believed in football like a new religion
And had perfect unquestioning faith in the fundamentals
Of blocking and tackling, the idea of warfare
Without suffering or death, the concept of teammates
Moving in harmony like the planets—and yet
Our awkward adolescent bodies were always canceling
The flawless beauty of Saturday afternoons in September,
Falling away from the particular grace of autumn,
The clear weather, the ideal game he imagined.
And so he drove us through punishing drills
On weekday afternoons, and doubled our practice time,
And challenged us to hammer him with forearms,
And devised elaborate, last-second plays—a flea-
Flicker, a triple reverse—to save us from defeat.
Almost always they worked. He despised losing
And loved winning more than his own body, maybe even
More than himself. But the last time I saw him
He looked wobbly and stunned by illness,
And I remembered the game in my senior year
When we met a downstate team who loved hitting
More than we did, who battered us all afternoon
With a vengeance, who destroyed us with timing
And power, with deadly, impersonal authority,
Machine-like fury, perfect execution.

Dojo

THOMAS CENTOLELLA

. . . . . .

If I'm stopped by the laughable
gaggle of little girls at the dojo,
wrapped in their white uniforms
of self-defense and working on their abs,
their ankles held down while they will
their tiny chins to their tiny knees—then

what gets me going again
is the lamentable
high school where I taught
a shy fifteen-year-old
the uses of metaphor, the magic
of calling one thing
by another's name,
and she taught me
in her small voice
to say the everyday straight out,
without reluctance or shame—
in her poem, "baby"
didn't mean "boyfriend"
or "sweetheart," it meant
baby, her baby—

a high school where mine
was the only light face
in a too full room of dark faces,
though I had my own darkness
and kept it to myself,
though they had their own light
and spent it freely, their hands
shooting high at every question,
bodies almost airborne, loud
entreaties for me to call on them,
to let them show off

how much they knew,
how worthy they were
of a hundred attentive ears—

a school that displays on the outside
a visionary's name
and on the inside: a metal detector,
heavy chains on the exit doors
(on the bars called "panic handles"),
and armed guards in uniforms
who have little use
for the clever turn of phrase,
the slangy wit, the heartfelt
sentiment—any lively song
that can make them forget
the world is a deadly place.

Brother Alvin

AUDRE LORDE

· · · · · ·

In the seat that we shared in the second grade
there was always a space between us
left for our guardian angels.
We had made it out of the brownies together
because you knew your numbers
and could find the right pages
while I could read all the words.
You were absent a lot between Halloween
and Thanksgiving
and just before Christmas vacation
you disappeared
along with the tinsel
and paper turkeys
and never returned.

My guardian angel and I had the seat to ourselves
for a little while only
until I was demoted back to the brownies
because I could never find the correct page.

You were not my first death,
but your going was not solaced by the usual
rituals of separation
the dark lugubrious murmurs
and invitations by threat
to the dignified grownups' view
of a child's inelegant pain
so even now
all these years of death later
I search through the index
of each new book
on magic
hoping to find some new spelling
of your name.

Teaching

AL YOUNG

. . . . . .

There's no such thing as a student,
only abiding faces unwilling
to change except with time,
the oldest force that still fools us

So you teach a feeling,
a notion learned the hard way,
a fact, some figures,
a tract, some rigors of childhood

The face out there
interacting with yours
knows how to grin & play with its pen
but misses the point so charmingly

A thousand moves later
that same shiny face
moving thru the world with
its eyes glazed or fully closed
reconnects with one of its own childhoods

Loosely we call this learning

Childhood Ideogram

LARRY LEVIS

. . . . . .

I lay my head sideways on the desk,
My fingers interlocked under my cheekbones,
My eyes closed. It was a three-room schoolhouse,
White, with a small bell tower, an oak tree.
From where I sat, on still days, I'd watch
The oak, the prisoner of that sky, or read
The desk carved with adults' names: Marietta
Martin, Truman Finnell, Marjorie Elm;
The wood hacked or lovingly hollowed, the flies
Settling on the obsolete & built-in inkwells.
I remember, tonight, only details, how
Mrs. Avery, now gone, was standing then
In her beige dress, its quiet, gazelle print
Still dark with lines of perspiration from
The day before; how Gracie Chin had just
Shown me how to draw, with chalk, a Chinese
Ideogram. Where did she go, white thigh
With one still freckle, lost in silk?
No one would say for sure, so that I'd know,
So that all shapes, for days after, seemed
Brushstrokes in Chinese: countries on maps
That shifted, changed colors, or disappeared:
Lithuania, Prussia, Bessarabia;
The numbers four & seven; the question mark.
That year, I ate almost nothing.
I thought my parents weren't my real parents,
I thought there'd been some terrible mistake.
At recess I would sit alone, seeing
In the print of each leaf shadow, an ideogram —
Still, indecipherable, beneath the green sound
The bell still made, even after it had faded,
When the dust-covered leaves of the oak tree
Quivered, slightly, if I looked up in time.
And my father, so distant in those days,

Where did he go, that autumn, when he chose
The chaste, faint ideogram of ash, & I had
To leave him there, white bones in a puzzle
By a plum tree, the sun rising over
The Sierras? It is not Chinese, but English —
When the past tense, when you first learn to use it
As a child, throws all the verbs in the language
Into the long, flat shade of houses you
Ride past, & into town. Your father's driving.
On winter evenings, the lights would come on earlier.
People would be shopping for Christmas. Each hand,
With the one whorl of its fingerprints, with twenty
Delicate bones inside it, reaching up
To touch some bolt of cloth, or choose a gift,
A little different from any other hand.
You know how the past tense turns a sentence dark,
But leaves names, lovers, places showing through:
Gracie Chin, my father, Lithuania;
A beige dress where dark gazelles hold still?
Outside, it's snowing, cold, & a New Year.
The trees & streets are turning white.
I always thought he would come back like this.
I always thought he wouldn't dare be seen.

Gratitude to Old Teachers

ROBERT BLY

. . . . . .

When we stride or stroll across the frozen lake,
We place our feet where they have never been.
We walk upon the unwalked. But we are uneasy.
Who is down there but our old teachers?

Water that once could take no human weight—
We were students then—holds up our feet,
And goes on ahead of us for a mile.
Beneath us the teachers, and around us the stillness.

School Days

WILLIAM MATTHEWS

. . . . . .

Once those fences kept me in. Mr. Mote
threw a dictionary at me in that room
on the corner, second floor, he and I
hypnotized by spite and everyone else
docile by default, for all we had was

fourth-grade manners: two gasped,
three tittered, Laneta hid her lovely head,
six palely watched their shoes as if they'd
brim and then flood urine, and the rest . . .
Good God, I'd forgot the rest. It's been

thirty-some years. That smart-ass afternoon
I loved them all and today all I can remember
is the name of one I loved and one I hated.
Wasn't he right to hurl at me a box
of words? By the time the dictionary spun

to rest under the radiator, its every page
was blank and the silent room was strewn
with print. I can't remember how we found
something to do, to bore up through that pall.
It would be as hard as that to remember

all their names—though, come to think of it,
I can. Isn't that how I got here,
and with you? I'm going to start at the north-
east corner of that hallucinated room
and name them one by one and row by row.

The Thing You Must Remember

MAGGIE ANDERSON

. . . . . .

The thing you must remember is how, as a child,
you worked hours in the art room, the teacher's
hands over yours, molding the little clay dog.
You must remember how nothing mattered
but the imagined dog's fur, the shape of his ears
and his paws. The gray clay felt dangerous,
your small hands were pressing what you couldn't
say with your limited words. When the dog's back
stiffened, then cracked to white shards
in the kiln, you learned how the beautiful
suffers from too much attention, how clumsy
a single vision can grow, and fragile
with trying too hard. The thing you must
remember is the art teacher's capable
hands: large, rough and grainy,
over yours, holding on.

The Schoolroom on the Second Floor of the Knitting Mill

JUDY PAGE HEITZMAN

. . . . . .

While most of us copied letters out of books,
Mrs. Lawrence carved and cleaned her nails.
Now the red and buff cardinals at my back-room window
make me miss her, her room, the hallway,
even the chimney outside
that broke up the sky.

In my memory it is afternoon.
Sun streams in through the door
next to the fire escape where we are lined up
getting our coats on to go out to the playground,
the tether ball, its towering height, the swings.
She tells me to make sure the line
does not move up over the threshold.
That would be dangerous.
So I stand guard at the door.
Somehow it happens
the way things seem to happen
when we're not really looking, or we are looking,
just not the right way.
Kids crush up like cattle, pushing me over the line.

Judy is not a good leader is all Mrs. Lawrence says.
She says it quietly. Still, everybody hears.
Her arms hang down like sausages.
I hear her every time I fail.

Schoolsville

BILLY COLLINS

· · · · · ·

Glancing over my shoulder at the past,
I realize the number of students I have taught
is enough to populate a small town.

I can see it nestled in a paper landscape,
chalk dust flurrying down in winter,
nights dark as a blackboard.

The population ages but never graduates.
On hot afternoons they sweat the final in the park
and when it's cold they shiver around stoves
reading disorganized essays out loud.
A bell rings on the hour and everybody zigzags
into the streets with their books.

I forgot all their last names first and their
first names last in alphabetical order.
But the boy who always had his hand up
is an alderman and owns the haberdashery.
The girl who signed her papers in lipstick
leans against the drugstore, smoking,
brushing her hair like a machine.

Their grades are sewn into their clothes
like references to Hawthorne.
The A's stroll along with other A's.
The D's honk whenever they pass another D.

All the creative writing students recline
on the courthouse lawn and play the lute.
Wherever they go, they form a big circle.

Needless to say, I am the mayor.
I live in the white colonial at Maple and Main.

I rarely leave the house. The car deflates
in the driveway. Vines twirl around the porch swing.

Once in a while a student knocks on the door
with a term paper fifteen years late
or a question about Yeats or double-spacing.
And sometimes one will appear in a windowpane
to watch me lecturing the wallpaper,
quizzing the chandelier, reprimanding the air.

Mrs. Krikorian

SHARON OLDS

· · · · · ·

She saved me. When I arrived in sixth grade,
a known criminal, the new teacher
asked me to stay after school the first day, she said
I've heard about you. She was a tall woman,
with a deep crevice between her breasts,
and a large, calm nose. She said,
This is a special library pass.
As soon as you finish your hour's work—
that hour's work that took ten minutes
and then the devil glanced into the room
and found me empty, a house standing open—
you can go to the library. Every hour
I'd zip through the work, and slip out of
my seat as if out of God's side and sail
down to the library, down through the empty
powerful halls, flash my pass
and stroll over to the dictionary
to look up the most interesting word
I knew, *spank*, dipping two fingers
into the jar of library paste to
suck that tart mucilage as I
came to the page with the cocker spaniel's
silks curling up like the fine steam of the body.
After *spank*, and *breast*, I'd move on
to *Abe Lincoln* and *Helen Keller*,
safe in their goodness till the bell, thanks
to Mrs. Krikorian, amiable giantess
with the kind eyes. When she asked me to write
a play, and direct it, and it was a flop,
and I hid in the coat-closet, she brought me a candy-cane
as you lay a peppermint on the tongue, and the worm
will come up out of the bowel to get it.
And so I was emptied of Lucifer
and filled with school glue and eros and

Amelia Earhart, saved by Mrs. Krikorian.
And who had saved Mrs. Krikorian?
When the Turks came across Armenia,
who slid her into the belly of a quilt, who
locked her in a chest, who mailed her to America?
And *that* one, who saved *her*, and *that* one—
who saved *her*, to save the one
who saved Mrs. Krikorian, who was
standing there on the sill of sixth grade, a
wide-hipped angel, smokey hair
standing up lightly all around her head?
I end up owing my soul to so many,
to the Armenian nation, one more soul someone
jammed behind a stove, drove
deep into a crack in a wall,
shoved under a bed. I would wake
up, in the morning, under my bed—not
knowing how I had got there—and lie
in the dusk, the dustballs beside my face
round and ashen, shining slightly
with the eerie comfort of what is neither good nor evil.

Drawing Hands

GREG WILLIAMSON

. . . . . .

Way on back in the reign of Mrs. Duke
All of the small subjects went in fear
Of her, her stormy eyes, her thunderhead
Of hair. Daily on the wall's clean slate,
She wrote the language he would learn to live
With: words and rules and examples of the rules
Whereby nouns adverbly verb their objects,
So that he might call things as he saw them.

There in the classroom, under a cloud of chalk,
How smoothly his attention used to glide
To the glass, to water braided on the glass,
Clearly clear, and standing still as it ran
Away, and deeper into the misted day
Where fields began dissolving into felt
And a stonefaced house reflected on the street.
Then the ruler would crack across his hand.

That boy lived my life ago, and whether
I leave him soloing at his desk today
Under the unbroken rules of Mrs. Duke
Or walking home through the mystifying day,
He finds his winding way back here somehow,
Where I sit high in the head of the house,
Writing and rewriting him, and watching the rain,
Which is what I came in out of for.

Zimmer in Grade School

PAUL ZIMMER

. . . . . .

In grade school I wondered
Why I had been born
To wrestle in the ashy puddles,
With my square nose
Streaming mucus and blood,
My knuckles puffed from combat
And the old nun's ruler.
I feared everything: God,
Learning and my schoolmates.
I could not count, spell or read.
My report card proclaimed
These scarlet failures.
My parents wrung their loving hands.
My guardian angel wept constantly.

But I could never hide anything.
If I peed my pants in class
The puddle was always quickly evident,
My worst mistakes were at
The blackboard for Jesus and all
The saints to see.
                   Even now
When I hide behind elaborate masks
It is always known that I am Zimmer,
The one who does the messy papers
And fractures all his crayons,
Who spits upon the radiators
And sits all day in shame
Outside the office of the principal.

The Boy in the Park

ROSEMARY WILLEY

. . . . . .

I was told not to touch him, not to let him
touch me, the head teacher explained how
he escaped into touch, the body's warmth,

slipping back through his six short years
to infancy, his limbs becoming slack.
But because Brian was happy he seemed less

lost than the other children. At a desk
behind a tall screen he'd crawl onto my lap
and rock with a deliberate rhythm.

I'd let my arms wrap around his curled back
and finish the song fragments he murmured
while he blinked up at me, surprised.

He could do the math, scrawling rote numbers
without a pause. I turned in the pages,
walked home wistful with the feeling of

Brian in my arms, like something you could
blow away or break. Nothing was so simple then
as the pang to love a strange child,

though today I flinch from the boy scuffing
in the park toward his mother, cradling his hands
like downed birds, just the way Brian did

before I'd press a pencil into his thin palm
and close the span of fingers. The truth is
I held him only once, afraid of getting caught,

of letting the others see my inability
to follow rules. I wanted him to remember me,
our afternoons, my name, though he could

not say it. That summer I wanted to say
goodbye but he broke from me, flailing his hands
and letting go a string of sounds above the park.

Mrs. Goldwasser

RON WALLACE

. . . . . .

Shimmered like butterscotch; the sun
had nothing on her. She bangled
when she walked. No one
did not love her. She shone,
she glowed, she lit up any room,
her every gesture jewelry.
And O, when she called us all by name
how we all performed!

Her string of little beads,
her pearls, her rough-cut
gemstones, diamonds, we hung
about her neck. And when
the future pressed her flat,
the world unclasped, and tarnished.

Mrs. Orton

RON WALLACE

. . . . . .

The perennial substitute, like some
obnoxious weed, a European interloper
in our native prairie, her instructions
full of nettles, her gestures parsnip
and burdock. Every day at 3:00 P.M.
we'd dig her out of our small lives,
and every morning she'd pop back.
We prayed she'd get the sack.

And to that end we taunted her—
tacks on her chair, a set-back clock—
as, weeping, she plodded through the week
turning, and turning the other cheek.
And every time we thought that we'd
eradicated her, she'd gone to seed.

Mr. Glusenkamp

RON WALLACE

. . . . . .

His gray face was a trapezoid, his voice
droned on like an ellipse.
He hated students and their noise
and loved the full eclipse
of their faces at the end of the day.
No one could have been squarer,
and nothing could have been plainer
than his geometry.

He didn't go for newfangled
stuff—new math, the open classroom.
And yet he taught us angles
and how lines intersect and bloom,
and how infinity was no escape,
and how to give abstractions shape.

Miss Goff

RON WALLACE

. . . . . .

When Zack Pulanski brought the plastic vomit
and slid it slickly to the vinyl floor
and raised his hand, and her tired eyes fell on it
with horror, the heartless classroom lost in laughter
as the custodian slyly tossed his saw dust on it
and pushed it, grinning, through the door,
she reached into her ancient corner closet
and found some Emily Dickinson mimeos there

which she passed out. And then, herself
passed out on the cold circumference of her desk.
And everybody went their merry ways
but me, who, chancing on one unexpected phrase
after another, sat transfixed until dusk.
Me and Miss Goff, the top of our heads taken off.

The Teacher

BRIGIT PEGEEN KELLY

. . . . . .

Still, still, still, the raven
flies up. His fingered
wings wagging as Mr. Foley's fingers
wag at the children. And he old in his teeth.
And he old in his knees. And knowing little
and helping no one. Only his fingers
wagging like a curtain going up
and a curtain going down.

In the low field
the cow with no hair on her knees
walks backwards under the locust tree. And the boy
Mr. Foley pointed at with his many fingers
waits for her. Stands in the flop
and waits, his hands full of powder
to free her of flies.

Mr. Foley killed this boy.
Or was it the bird? Or was Mr. Foley
the bird? The bird who broke
the boy's knees? The boy
wept in his hair. In his arm.
So ashamed, so lonely, without water or clothes.

Still, still, still, the willow
says forgive. The boy
may be planted in the field. Perhaps
he will grow like a fence or a tree
and the tent worms will build him their nests—
string their white wings
from his heart, from his heels,
and he will be halfway
to heaven and up.

Notes on Contributors

KATHLEEN AGUERO is the author of two books of poems, most recently *The Real Weather*. She is the editor of *Daily Fare: Essays from the Multicultural Experience* and coeditor of *An Ear to the Ground: An Anthology of Contemporary American Poetry*. Aguero has been a poet-in-residence in many schools in New Hampshire and Massachusetts. Currently she teaches at Pine Manor College in Chestnut Hill, Massachusetts.

SHERMAN ALEXIE is the author of ten books, most recently a novel, *Indian Killer*, and a collection of poems, *The Summer of Black Widows*. His book *Reservation Blues* won an American Book Award from the Before Columbus Foundation. Alexie is also the author of *The Lone Ranger and Tonto Fistfight in Heaven*, which served as the basis for his screenplay for the film *Smoke Signals*, winner of two Sundance Film Festival Awards in 1998. Sherman Alexie is a Spokane and Coeur d'Alene Indian from Wellpinit, Washington.

DICK ALLEN is the author of five books of poems including *Flight and Pursuit* and *Ode to the Cold War: Poems New and Selected*. In the late 1970s he founded and ran the statewide Young Writers Awards Competition for all high school students in Connecticut through the University of Bridgeport, where he currently teaches and directs the creative writing program. He has also served as a mentor in the Connecticut Young Writers program since its inception.

MAGGIE ANDERSON, coeditor of *Learning by Heart*, is the author of four books of poems, most recently *A Space Filled with Moving*. She is also the editor of *Hill Daughter: New and Selected Poems* by West Virginia poet Louise McNeill (1911–1993), and coeditor of *A Gathering of Poets*, an anthology of poetry commemorating the shootings of students in 1970 at Kent State University and Jackson State. Anderson teaches at Kent State University where she directs the Wick Poetry Program and edits a poetry series through the Kent State University Press. She taught from 1979 to 1989 in schools, prisons, hospitals, and senior centers and continues to conduct workshops for teachers.

RANE ARROYO's most recent book of poems is *Pale Ramón*. His book *The Singing Shark* won the 1997 Carl Sandburg Poetry

Prize. Arroyo teaches at the University of Toledo in Toledo, Ohio. He has worked as a program associate for Urban Gateways in Chicago, teaching and hiring residency artists for Chicago public schools.

JAN BEATTY is the 1995 winner of the Agnes Lynch Starrett Poetry Prize for her book, *Mad River*. She has taught for eight years at colleges and universities in the Pittsburgh, Pennsylvania, area and for two years in the International Poetry Forum's Poets-in-Person program in Pittsburgh high schools.

ROBIN BECKER is the author of four books of poems including *Giacometti's Dog* and *All-American Girl*, which won the 1997 Lambda Literary Award in Lesbian Poetry. She currently teaches in the M.F.A. in Writing program at Pennsylvania State University and is the poetry editor of *The Women's Review of Books*.

ROBERT BLY is a poet, translator, and lecturer. He is the author of nine volumes of poetry, most recently *Morning Poems*. He is also the author of the best-selling *Iron John*, and coeditor of the anthology *The Rag and Bone Shop of the Heart*. For many years, he was the editor of the magazine *The Fifties* (later *The Sixties* and *The Seventies*), in which he published major European and South American poets for the first time in English translation.

He has long been involved, as a teacher and speaker, with the development of the men's movement in the United States.

RICHARD BRAUTIGAN's first novel, *A Confederate General from Big Sur*, was published in 1965. He is also the author of *Trout Fishing in America*, *In Watermelon Sugar*, and a collection of poems, *The Pill Versus the Springhill Mine Disaster*. He died in 1984.

GWENDOLYN BROOKS was the first black poet to win a Pulitzer Prize (1950). In 1968 she succeeded Carl Sandburg as Poet Laureate of Illinois. As poet laureate, Brooks sponsors many activities and contests for schoolchildren including the annual Gwendolyn Brooks Poetry Awards. Brooks is the author of many books, including poetry for adults and children, one novel, and an autobiography, and she has received over fifty honorary degrees and numerous other awards. Her most recent books are *Children Coming Home*, a collection of poems, and *Report from Part Two*, the second half of her autobiography.

JEANNE BRYNER is the author of *Breathless*, which won the 1995 Wick Poetry Chapbook Prize. Her poems have been published in many magazines and anthologies including *Between the Heartbeats: An Anthology of Poetry and Prose by Nurses*. Bryner works as a resident nurse in the emergency room at Trumbull Memorial Hospital in Warren, Ohio. She has taught poetry workshops at West Virginia University, in Ohio schools, and at a camp for surviving children of cancer victims.

CHRISTOPHER BURSK teaches at Bucks County Community College in Pennsylvania and has been, since 1978, the Poet Laureate of Bucks County. He is the author of seven books of poems, most recently *One True Religion*. Bursk has taught poetry workshops in a correctional facility and a center for the aging. He was awarded the Pennsylvania Professor of the Year and National Silver Medal by the Council for the Advancement and Support of Education in 1991.

BRENDA CÁRDENAS is the author of a chapbook, *Weaving Generations*, and has published poems in many magazines including *Prairie Schooner* and *ViAztlán: A Journal of Arts and Letters*. She is a certified high school teacher and has taught English at Menomonee Falls High School and Spanish at Chilton High School in Wisconsin. Currently, she teaches English courses in the Comprehensive Studies Program, a minority retention program at the University of Michigan in Ann Arbor.

CYRUS CASSELLS is the author of four books of poems including *Soul Make a Path through Shouting* and *Beautiful Signor*. Cassells is also the author of two

plays and of *Bayok*, a short film on Filipino-American dancer Gregory Silva. He has been a poet-in-residence at a private middle school in Hillsborough, California, and has also taught at many colleges and universities. Currently he teaches at Southwest Texas State University near Austin.

ROSEMARY CATACALOS is the author of a full-length collection of poems, *Again for the First Time*, and of a handmade letterpress chapbook, *As Long as It Takes*. The former director of the San Francisco Poetry Center, Catacalos also worked for ten years as a poet-in-the-schools in the San Antonio Independent School District where she herself attended grades four through twelve.

THOMAS CENTOLELLA has taught poetry writing to grades kindergarten through twelve since 1986 through the California Poets-in-the-Schools program. He also teaches writing at the College of Marin north of San Francisco and is a staff artist for the Goldman Institute on Aging. His two collections of poems are *Lights & Mysteries* and *Terra Firma*.

BARBARA CLEARY is coauthor of two books on pedagogy, *Orchestrating Learning with Quality* and *Tools and Techniques to Inspire Classroom Learning*. She began her teaching career at Black Rock School in Bridgeport, Connecticut, and has taught English at the Miami Valley School in Dayton, Ohio, for twenty-five years.

LISA COFFMAN won the 1995 Stan and Tom Wick Poetry Prize for her first book, *Likely*. She has taught in the Trenton, New Jersey, YWCA After-School-in-the-Arts program and at several colleges and universities including New York University, Deep Springs College, and Pennsylvania State University at Altoona.

MICHAEL COLLIER is the author of three books of poems, most recently *The Neighbor*, and he is the editor of *The Wesleyan Tradition: Four Decades of American Poetry*. Collier teaches at the University of Maryland and Warren Wilson College and serves as the conference director for the Bread Loaf Writers Conference. He also conducts an after-school book club at his son's elementary school and regularly visits Baltimore area high schools to speak with students about poetry.

BILLY COLLINS is the author of six books of poems, most recently *Picnic, Lightning*. He has received many awards for his poetry and in 1992 he was chosen by the New York Public Library to serve as a Literary Lion. Collins has conducted summer poetry workshops in Ireland at University College Galway and he teaches at Lehman College, CUNY.

JIM DANIELS is the author of four books of poems, most recently *Blessing the House*, and he is the editor of *Letters to America: Contemporary American Poetry on Race*. For twelve years Daniels taught as a poet-in-the-schools in Michigan. He currently teaches at Carnegie-Mellon University in Pittsburgh, Pennsylvania, and has conducted poetry workshops for the Governor's School for the Arts and the Western Pennsylvania School for the Deaf.

ANN DARR graduated valedictorian from a one-building elementary and secondary school in Bagley, Iowa, in 1937. She is the author of eight books of poems including *The Myth of a Woman's Fist* and *Flying the Zuni Mountains*. From 1955 to 1997 she taught as a poet-in-the-schools in Maryland and Virginia. She has been a poet-in-residence with the American Wind Symphony aboard *Point Counterpoint II* in towns along East Coast rivers and the Mississippi.

TOI DERRICOTTE's most recent book of poems is *Tender* and her prose book, *The Black Notebooks: An Interior Journey*, was published in 1997. She also coauthored *Creative Writing: A Manual for Teachers* for the New Jersey State Council on the Arts where she served as a Master Teacher from 1973 to 1988. For three years Derricotte was an educational consultant through Columbia University, working with boards of education and teachers on equality in education. With Cornelius Eady she founded and implemented Cave Canem, the first historic workshop and retreat for African American poets. Derricotte currently teaches in the M.F.A. in Writing program at the University of Pittsburgh.

CHITRA BANERJEE DIVAKARUNI is the author of a novel, *The Mistress of Spices*, a collection of stories, *Arranged Marriage*, and four books of poems, most recently *Leaving Yuba City*. Born in India, Divakaruni now teaches at Foothill College in the San Francisco Bay Area. She has won many awards for her fiction and poetry including an American Book Award from the Before Columbus Foundation. Divakaruni is also one of the founders of MAITRI, a help line for South Asian women in the Bay Area, and currently serves as its president.

GREGORY DJANIKIAN's most recent book of poems is *About Distance*. He is currently the director of creative writing at the University of Pennsylvania. For five years, he taught as a poet-in-the-schools in central New York State. Djanikian attended kindergarten through second grade in Alexandria, Egypt, and then attended schools in Williamsport, Pennsylvania, and Albany, California.

PATRICIA DOBLER is the author of three books including *Talking to Strangers*, which won the 1986 Brittingham Poetry Prize, and *UXB*, a collection of poems and of translations from the German of Ilse Aichinger. She has been a poet-in-the-schools in Pennsylvania and is currently director of the Women's Creative Writing Center at Carlow College in Pittsburgh.

MARK DOTY is the author of five books of poems, mostly recently *Atlantis* and *Sweet Machine*. He is also the author of a memoir, *Heaven's Coast*. Before his current teaching position at the University of Utah, Doty worked as a Head Start teacher, a preschool teacher, a Before-and-After-School program teacher, as the director of a federally-funded day care center, and as a poet-in-residence in the Iowa Artists-in-the-Schools program.

RITA DOVE served as Poet Laureate of the United States and Consultant in Poetry to the Library of Congress from 1993 to 1995. She has received numerous literary and academic honors, among them the 1987 Pulitzer Prize in Poetry for *Thomas and Beulah*. Dove has published five books of poems, a book of short stories, *Fifth Sunday*, the novel *Through the Ivory Gate*, a collection of essays, and the play, *The Darker Face of the Earth*. Dove was a Presidential Scholar, one of the top 100 high school graduates in the United States in 1970. Currently, she teaches at the University of Virginia in Charlottesville.

STEPHEN DUNN is the author of ten collections of poetry, most recently *Loosestrife*, and two books of prose including *Riffs & Reciprocities*. He has taught for twenty-four years at Richard Stockton College in New Jersey. For nine years Dunn taught as a poet-in-the-schools in Minnesota and New Jersey.

CORNELIUS EADY's five books of poems include *Victims of the Latest Dance Craze*, which won the 1985 Lamont Prize from the Academy of American Poets, and *The Autobiography of a Jukebox*. He has taught at Sarah Lawrence College in New York, the Writer's Voice, the 92nd Street Y, and Sweet Briar College and he currently teaches at SUNY Stony Brook. With Toi Derricotte, he founded and implemented Cave Canem, the first historic workshop and retreat for African American poets.

THOMAS SAYERS ELLIS's chapbook *The Good Junk* was published as a part of *Take Three: Agni New Poets Series # 1*. His poems have been published in many magazines and anthologies including *Callaloo, Best American Poetry 1997*, and the *1998 Pushcart Prize XXII*. Ellis currently teaches English and African American Studies at Case Western Reserve University in Cleveland, Ohio.

LOUISE ERDRICH is a member of the Turtle Mountain Chippewa tribe. She attended the Wahpeton Indian Boarding School in North Dakota, where both her parents taught. After graduating from Dartmouth College in 1976, Erdrich returned to North Dakota and taught in the Poetry-in-the-Schools program. She is the author of five novels, including *Love Medicine, Tracks, Tales of Burning Love*, and *The Antelope Wife*. Her two books of poems are *Jacklight* and *Baptism of Desire*.

MARTÍN ESPADA was born and attended public schools in Brooklyn, New York. He has published five books of poems, most recently *City of Coughing and Dead Radiators* and *Imagine the Angels of Bread*, which won an American Book Award from the Before Columbus Foundation. He has taught grades six through eight in the Agassiz School in Cambridge, Massachusetts; in the Worcester County House of Corrections in Boylston, Massachusetts; and in various adult literacy programs through the P.E.N. Readers & Writers program in New York City. Espada currently teaches at the University of Massachusetts at Amherst.

DAVE ETTER is the author of twenty-five books of poems, including *Central Standard Time, Alliance, Illinois*, and *West of Chicago*, which won the Carl Sandburg Poetry Prize. Etter has been a freelance writer and editor for many years and has also taught poetry workshops at various colleges and universities and in the Illinois and Missouri Poets-in-the-Schools programs.

DIANE GILLIAM FISHER's chapbook of poems, *Recipe for Blackberry Cake*, won the 1997 Wick Poetry Chapbook Prize. She has published poems in *Appalachian Heritage*, *Now & Then*, and *Crab Orchard Review*. Fisher attended Eakin Elementary and other public schools in Columbus and Westerville, Ohio.

PHIL GEORGE is a member of the Nez Perce tribe and has published his poems in many magazines and anthologies including *Whispering Winds*, *The Remembered Earth*, and the *Idaho Poetry Anthology*. He also wrote, narrated, and coproduced the National Public Broadcasting program "Season of the Grandmothers." George has taught Pacific Northwest Indian history and heritage in public schools in Spokane, Takoma, and Seattle, Washington. In 1970 he won first place in the National Fancy Dance Championship sponsored by the National Indian Athletic Association.

GARY GILDNER is the author of more than fifteen books including poetry, fiction, and memoirs. His most recent book of poems, *The Bunker in the Parsley Fields*, won the Iowa Poetry Award in 1997. In the formative years of the poets-in-the-schools programs, Gildner visited schools and conducted master classes in Iowa, Minnesota, South Dakota, Kansas, and Colorado. He has been a writer-in-residence at Michigan State University and Reed College, and has taught at universities in the former Czechoslovakia and in Poland.

MEL GLENN has taught English for nearly thirty years at the high school from which he graduated, Abraham Lincoln High School in Brooklyn, New York. In the 1960s Glenn taught high school English and history in Sierra Leone, West Africa. He has published many books of poetry written in the voices of his students, including *Class Dismissed*, *Back to Class*, *The Taking of Room 114*, and *Jump Ball*.

LOUISE GLÜCK is the author of seven books of poems including *Meadowlands* and *The Wild Iris*, which won the Pulitzer Prize for Poetry in 1993. She is also the author of *Proofs & Theories: Essays on Poetry*. Glück has taught at the University of California at Berkeley, Columbia, the University of Iowa, and at Williams College in Massachusetts where she has an ongoing appointment.

SARA GOODRICH was home schooled through the seventh grade, attended one year of high school, and graduated at age sixteen after taking the California High School Challenge exam. She is currently eighteen years old and is serving in the U.S. Navy.

JORIE GRAHAM is the author of five books of poems including *The Errancy* and *The Dream of the Unified Field: Selected Poems 1974–1994*, which won the Pulitzer Prize for Poetry in 1995. Graham teaches at the University of Iowa Writer's Workshop and has received many awards for her writing including the John D. and Catherine T. MacArthur Fellowship.

EAMON GRENNAN was born in Ireland and attended a boarding school in Roscrea, County Tipperary, run by Cistercian monks. He attended college and university in Ireland and then in the United States. Grennan's most recent books of poems are *So It Goes* and *Relations: New and Selected Poems*. He has taught for many years at Vassar College in Poughkeepsie, New York.

MAURICE KILWEIN GUEVARA was born in Belencito, Colombia, and was raised in Pittsburgh, Pennsylvania. He is the author of two books of poems, *Postmortem* and *Poems of the River Spirit*. He is also featured in *Touching the Fire: Fifteen Poets of Today's Latino Renaissance*, edited by Ray Gonzalez. Guevara taught for five years as a poet-in-the-schools and he currently teaches creative writing at Indiana University of Pennsylvania.

RICHARD HAGUE is the author of five books of poems, most recently *A Bestiary* and *Mill and Smoke Marrow*. He is also the author of *Mill Town Natural: Essays and Stories from a Life.* Since 1969 Hague has taught high school English classes at Purcell Marian High School in Cincinnati, Ohio. The writing program he designed and directed at Purcell Marian won first place in the United States in the 1994 Excellence in English Awards given by the English-Speaking Union.

DONALD HALL is the author of many books of poems, essays, short stories, textbooks, and books for children and young adults. His thirteenth book of poems, *Without*, was published in 1998. Hall attended Spring Glen Grammar School in New Hampshire. He taught from 1957 to 1975 at the University of Michigan in Ann Arbor.

JAMES HARMS is the author of two books of poems, *Modern Ocean* and *The Joy Addict*. He has worked as a substitute teacher in the Glendale, Burbank, and Lawndale, California, Public School Systems. Harms has taught at Denison University, the University of Redlands, and Indiana University, and he currently teaches at West Virginia University.

MARC HARSHMAN has been, until recently, a grade-school teacher in Marshall County, West Virginia, teaching the fifth and sixth grades at Sand Hill School, one of the last of the three-room country schools. He is the author of seven children's books, including *The Storm*, a Smithsonian Notable Book for Children and a Parents' Choice Award recipient. His chapbook of poems, *Turning Out the Stones*, won the State Street Poetry Prize. As a children's author, Harshman frequently visits schools throughout the eastern United States.

DAVID HASSLER, coeditor of *Learning by Heart*, is the author of *Sabishi: poems from japan*, which won the 1993 Wick Poetry Chapbook Prize. He is the editor of *April Seeds Dreaming of Sky*, an anthology of poetry by first and second graders. With his wife, Lynn Gregor, he has coedited *A Place To Grow: Voices and Images of Urban Gardeners*. He works as a poet-in-the-schools for the Ohio Arts Council and is an Associate Artist for the Shaker Heights High School Theatre Department in Cleveland, Ohio. With his Shaker Theatre students, he has presented their original writing and performances at National Council of Teachers of English regional and national conferences.

JUDY PAGE HEITZMAN has taught English at Duxbury High School in Duxbury, Massachusetts, since 1975. Her book of poems, *Maybe Grace*, won the Sandstone Poetry Book Contest in 1993 and her poetry has been published in many magazines including *Yankee* and *The New Yorker*.

CONRAD HILBERRY's most recent book of poems is *Sorting the Smoke: New and Selected Poems*. He has taught for many years at Kalamazoo College and in the Michigan Poets-in-the-Schools program.

EDWARD HIRSCH is the author of five books of poems, most recently *Earthly Measures* and *On Love*. He has taught poetry writing at every level of elementary and secondary school and he now teaches in the creative writing program at the University of Houston.

DAVID HUDDLE is the author of ten books of poetry, fiction, and essays. His most recent collection is *Summer Lake: New and Selected Poems*. Huddle has taught for twenty-six years at the University of Vermont and has conducted fourteen sessions of the Bread Loaf School of English.

T. R. HUMMER's books of poems include *The Passion of the Right-Angled Man, Lower-Class Heresy*, and *Walt Whitman in Hell*. He worked as a poet-in-the-schools in Mississippi during the 1970s and was the state coordinator for Artists-in-Schools for the Mississippi Arts Commission from 1974 to 1977. Hummer also taught a creative writing course at Point of the Mountain State Prison in Utah. He currently teaches at Virginia Commonwealth University in Richmond.

PAUL B. JANECZKO worked for twenty-two years as a high school English teacher until 1991, when he left teaching to work as a visiting poet. He is the editor of more than twenty poetry anthologies for young people including *Preposterous: Poems of Youth*, *The Music of What Happens*, and *Going Over to Your Place*. With Naomi Shihab Nye, he edited *I Feel a Little Jumpy Around You*. In addition, Janeczko is the author of eight books of poetry, fiction, and nonfiction including *Brickyard Summer* and *Sparks and Wonder: Teaching Kids to Write Poetry*.

ALLISON JOSEPH is the author of three books of poems, most recently *Soul Train* and *In Every Seam*. She currently teaches at Southern Illinois University at Carbondale, where she is the poetry editor of *Crab Orchard Review*. Joseph was born in London, England, to parents of Caribbean heritage. She grew up in Toronto, Canada, and the Bronx, New York, and is a graduate of the Bronx High School of Science.

JULIA KASDORF's first collection of poems, *Sleeping Preacher*, won the 1991 Agnes Lynch Starrett Poetry Prize. Her second book, *Eve's Striptease*, was published in 1998. Kasdorf has taught business English at St. Anthony Commercial School in New York City and was a tutor of English

as a second language in the United States and China in 1982. She currently teaches writing at Messiah College in Pennsylvania.

BRIGIT PEGEEN KELLY won the 1987 Yale Series of Younger Poets Prize for *To the Place of Trumpets*. Her second collection of poems, *Song*, was published in 1995. Kelly has worked as a poet-in-the-schools in Oregon and through the Dodge Foundation in New Jersey. She currently teaches creative writing at the University of Illinois.

JANE KENYON was born in Ann Arbor, Michigan, in 1947. She published four collections of poetry and translated the poetry of Anna Akhmatova. Kenyon was featured with her husband, Donald Hall, in the Emmy Award–winning Bill Moyers special, "A Life Together." Jane Kenyon died in April 1995. Her new and selected poems, *Otherwise*, was published posthumously in 1996.

KENNETH KOCH's *Wishes, Lies and Dreams* and *Rose, Where Did You Get That Red?*, both first published in the 1970s, are classics in the literature of teaching poetry to children. He is the author of many books of poetry, most recently *Straits* and *One Train*. His nonfiction books include *The Art of Poetry* and *Making Your Own Days: The Pleasures of Reading and Writing Poetry*. Koch has taught poetry in elementary and secondary schools in the United States, France, Italy, and China, and he currently teaches at Columbia University.

FRANK KOOISTRA's poems have been published in *The Hawaii Review*, *Pudding Magazine*, *Pleiades*, and other magazines. He has taught at the University of Alberta in Canada and at the University of Akron and Kent State University in Ohio.

MAXINE KUMIN has published eleven volumes of poetry as well as novels, short stories, and essays on country living, most recently *Women, Animals, and Vegetables*. She was awarded the Pulitzer Prize in Poetry in 1973 for *Up Country* and her *Collected Poems* was published in 1998. Kumin has been a Consultant in Poetry to the Library of Congress and she is a chancellor of the Academy of American Poets and Poet Laureate of New Hampshire. She worked as a poet-in-the-schools in Washington, D.C., in the beginning years of the program.

DORIANNE LAUX is the author of two books of poems, *Awake* and *What We Carry*. With Kim Addonizio, she edited *The Poet's Companion: A Guide to the Pleasures of Writing Poetry*. From 1984 to 1990 Laux taught in the California Poets-in-the-Schools program and the California Heritage program. In 1997 she wrote the introduction to the California Poets-in-the-

Schools statewide anthology, *Belonging to California*. She currently teaches at the University of Oregon.

LI-YOUNG LEE was born in Jakarta, Indonesia, and attended public schools in western Pennsylvania. He is the author of two volumes of poetry, *Rose* and *The City in Which I Love You*, and a memoir, *The Winged Seed*. Lee conducts poetry workshops and does readings throughout the country, including visits to his children's elementary school in Chicago.

PHILIP LEVINE's recent books of poetry include *What Work Is*, winner of the 1991 National Book Award, *The Simple Truth*, and *Unselected Poems*. He is also the author of *The Bread of Time: Toward an Autobiography*. Levine was educated in the Detroit public schools and at Wayne University (now Wayne State University). He taught at California State University at Fresno for many years, until his recent retirement.

LARRY LEVIS attended public schools in Fresno, California, and California State University at Fresno. He published five collections of poems during his life, most recently *The Widening Spell of the Leaves*, as well as a collection of stories, *Black Freckles*. At the time of his death in 1996, Levis taught at Virginia Commonwealth University in Richmond, and he had taught previously at the University of Missouri, the University of Iowa, and the Warren Wilson College Creative Writing program. Larry Levis's posthumous collection of poems, *Elegy*, was published in 1997 with a foreword by Philip Levine.

JULIA LISELLA's poems have been published in several magazines and anthologies, including *For A Living: The Poetry of Work* and *Unsettling America: An Anthology of Contemporary Multicultural Poetry*. She has taught English as a second language and composition at Tufts University in Massachusetts; poetry and nonfiction at New York University; poetry at Goldwater Memorial Hospital in New York City; and journalism at Junior High 125 in Sunnyside, Queens.

CHRIS LLEWELLYN's book, *Fragments from the Fire: The Triangle Shirtwaist Company Fire of March 25, 1911*, won the Walt Whitman Award from the Academy of American Poets in 1986. Her second book of poems, *Steam Dummy*, was published in 1993. Llewellyn has taught poetry at The Writers' Center in Bethesda, Maryland, and through Writerscorps/Americorps at public schools, hospitals, and recreation centers in Washington D.C.

AUDRE LORDE was born in Harlem and attended Hunter College High School. While a high school student, she joined the Harlem Writers' Guild founded by John Henrick Clarke. Lorde was the cofounder, with Barbara Smith, of Kitchen Table: Women of Color Press. The author of ten books of poems and five books of prose, Lorde worked as a librarian for eight years before beginning her teaching career. At the time of her death in 1992, she was Thomas Hunter Professor of English at Hunter College in New York City and was named New York State Poet. *The Collected Poems of Audre Lorde* was published in 1998.

WILLIAM MATTHEWS was the author of twelve books of poems, including *Blues if You Want, Selected Poems and Translations*, and *Time & Money*, for which he won the National Book Critics Circle Award for Poetry in 1995. In 1996 he was awarded the Ruth Lilly Prize by the Modern Poetry Association. William Matthews died in November 1997. A new collection of poems, *After All: Last Poems*, was published posthumously in 1998.

LINDA MCCARRISTON is the author of two books of poems, *Talking Soft Dutch* and *Eva-Mary*, which won the 1991 Terrence Des Pres Prize in Poetry. She has taught English at public high schools and junior highs in Massachusetts and New York, and she toured as a poet for the National Book Foundation in Vermont Public Schools. McCarriston has also taught at the Bread Loaf Young Writers Conference in

Middlebury, Vermont, and currently teaches at the University of Alaska, Anchorage.

COLLEEN J. MCELROY's books of poetry include *What Madness Brought Me Here: Collected Poems, 1968–88, Bone Flames,* and *Queen of the Ebony Isles,* which won an American Book Award from the Before Columbus Foundation. She is also the author of a collection of short stories and a travel memoir, *A Long Way from St. Louie,* published in 1997. McElroy teaches at the University of Washington in Seattle, and she has been a poet-in-residence and a master poet and mentor in the Seattle public schools.

PEG MCNALLY's poetry has been published in the anthology *Microfiction* and in *Southeast Review.* She teaches at Robert H. Jamison Junior High School in Cleveland, Ohio.

KYOKO MORI was born in Japan and is the author of two novels, *Shizuko's Daughter* and *One Bird.* She is also the author of two nonfiction works, *The Dream of Water: A Memoir* and *Polite Lies: On Being a Woman Caught Between Cultures.* Her book of poetry, *Fallout,* was published in 1994. Mori has taught since 1984 at St. Norbert College in De Pere, Wisconsin.

SUSAN MURRAY graduated from Shaker Heights High School in Cleveland, Ohio, in 1997. While a student, she had four original works staged and produced by Shaker Theatre in its New Stages Playwrights' Series. Her play, *Lost City of Cleveland,* was a finalist for the New York Young Playwrights' Festival in 1997. Murray is currently a student in the playwrighting program at Carnegie-Mellon University in Pittsburgh, Pennsylvania.

MARILYN NELSON is the author of five books of poems, most recently, *For the Body* and *In the Fields of Praise: New and Selected Poems.* She has given readings and workshops at public schools and teaches at the University of Connecticut at Storrs.

NAOMI SHIHAB NYE has been working as an itinerant writer-in-the-schools and visiting writer-at-large for the past twenty-four years, especially in Texas. Nye is the author of a novel, several picture books for children, and the editor of five poetry anthologies for young readers, including *I Feel A Little Jumpy Around You,* which she coedited with Paul Janeczko. She is the author of seven books of poems, most recently *Words Under the Words: Selected Poems* and *Fuel.* Her collection of essays, *Never in a Hurry: Essays on People and Places,* was published in 1996.

JOYCE CAROL OATES has, since 1980, published more than twenty-five novels and short story collections, in addition to several volumes of poetry. Her most recent novels are *My Heart Laid Bare* and *Man Crazy*. *Tenderness and Other Poems* was published in 1996. She has taught writing and literature at the university level since 1963. Oates currently teaches at Princeton University.

FRANK O'HARA published several books of poems between 1952 and 1964, including *Meditations in an Emergency* and *Lunch Poems*. His *Collected Poems*, edited by Donald Allen, was published in 1971. O'Hara was also the author of more than 100 essays, reviews, and catalog introductions. He lived in New York City and worked as a curator for the Museum of Modern Art until his death in 1966.

SHARON OLDS is the author of five books of poems, most recently *The Wellspring*, published in 1996. She has won many awards for her poetry including the 1983 Lamont Poetry Prize from the Academy of American Poets and the National Book Critics Circle Award for *The Dead and the Living*. Olds teaches at New York University and helps to run a writing workshop in a 900-bed New York City hospital for the severely disabled.

CAROL OLES is the author of five books of poems, most recently *The Deed* and *Stunts*. She has worked as a substitute high school English teacher in Queens, New York, and has taught English as a foreign language at the American School in Tangier, Morocco. Oles has also worked as a poet-in-the-schools (kindergarten through twelfth grades) in Massachusetts. She currently teaches at California State University in Chico.

RON PADGETT is the author of more than twenty-five books of poems and books on education. He also has translated the poetry and fiction of Guillaume Apollinaire and the *Complete Poems of Blaise Cendrars*. Padgett's *New and Selected Poems* was published in 1995. He is the coeditor with David Shapiro of *An Anthology of New York Poets* and editor of *The Complete Poems of Edwin Denby*. A founding member of the Teachers and Writers Collaborative in New York City, Padgett has taught for thirty years in poetry-in-the-schools programs in many states. He is currently the director of publications for the Teachers and Writers Collaborative.

LINDA PASTAN's tenth book of poems, *Carnival Evening: New and Selected Poems 1968–1998*, was published in 1998. Her other books of poems include *Aspects of Eve*, *The Five Stages of Grief*, and *Heroes in Disguise*. Pastan was named Poet Laureate of Maryland in 1991.

MOLLY PEACOCK is the author of four books of poems, most recently *Original Love*, published in 1995. In 1998 she published a memoir, *Paradise, Piece by Piece*. She taught in the poets-in-the-schools program during the 1970s and worked for more than ten years as a middle school teacher and learning specialist at Friends Seminary School in New York City.

HILDA RAZ's most recent book of poems, *Divine Honors*, was published in 1997. Her poems have been published in many anthologies, including *Cancer through the Eyes of Ten Women* and *The Bread Loaf Anthology of Contemporary Nature Poetry*. She is the editor-in-chief of the literary quarterly *Prairie Schooner*, and teaches at the University of Nebraska–Lincoln. Raz worked in the artist-in-the-schools program of the Nebraska Arts Council for fifteen years.

CLENN REED's poems have been published in *Alaska Quarterly Review, Ploughshares, Faultline Review*, and other magazines. He has worked as a substitute teacher for the Westchester County, New York, public schools. Reed has also taught at Long Island University in Brooklyn, Mercy College in Dobbs Ferry, New York, and Sarah Lawrence College in Bronxville, New York.

JOHN REPP's book, *Thirst Like This*, won the Devins Award for Poetry from the University of Missouri Press in 1990. He is the editor of *How We Live Now: Contemporary Multicultural Lit-*

erature, and his recent poems have been published in *Kenyon Review, The Iowa Review*, and *Puerto del Sol*. He currently teaches at Edinboro University of Pennsylvania.

SONIA SANCHEZ is the author of more than fifteen books of poetry, plays, and books for children. Her books of poems include *Does Your House Have Lions?* and *homegirls and handgrenades*, for which Sanchez won an American Book Award from the Before Columbus Foundation in 1985. She is the coeditor with Ed Bullins of *New Plays from the Black Theater* and editor of *Three Hundred and Sixty Degrees of Blackness Come at You* and *Twenty-five Stories of Black Americans*. Sanchez has taught at Temple University in Philadelphia since 1977.

JEANNE SHANNON is the author of two poetry chapbooks, *Dissolving Forms* and *Moon of Changing Seasons*. Her poems have been published in several magazines and in the anthology *Party Train: A Collection of North American Prose Poetry*. Shannon was a student teacher in choral music and French at Pulaski High School in Pulaski, Virginia, and in 1956–1957, she taught sixth grade at Pound Elementary School in Pound, Virginia.

BETSY SHOLL is the author of five books of poems, most recently *The Red Line* and *Don't Explain*.

She taught for one year at Kings Preparatory, a Catholic high school in Rochester, New York. Sholl has also taught in many poets-in-the-schools programs and conducted workshops in prisons. Recently she has taught in the Vermont College M.F.A. in Writing program and at the University of Pittsburgh.

THOMAS R. SMITH is the author of two collections of poetry, *Keeping the Star* and *Horse of Earth*. He has conducted poetry workshops in schools and often visited schools during his tenure as director of Artspeople, a community arts organization in western Wisconsin.

GARY SNYDER is the author of many books of poems and prose, including a collection of essays, *The Practice of the Wild*, and *No Nature: New and Selected Poems*. Snyder's *Mountains and Rivers Without End*, a book-length poem, was published in 1996. He has taught English in Japan, and he currently teaches at the University of California at Davis.

GARY SOTO is the author of twenty-six books for adults and young readers, including *Elements of San Joaquin*, *Where Sparrows Work Hard*, *Novio Boy*, and *Chato's Kitchen*. He is also the author of two books of prose, *Living Up the Street: Narrative Recollections*, and *Small Faces*. He has produced two films for Spanish-speaking children and

is an officer in the Royal Chicano Navy, based in Fresno.

WILLIAM STAFFORD was the author of more than thirty-five books of poetry and prose, including *Passwords* and *Writing the Australian Crawl: Views on the Writer's Vocation*. He won the National Book Award for poetry for *Traveling through the Dark*. Stafford taught at Lewis and Clark College in Portland, Oregon, until his death in 1993. Two new books were published posthumously in 1998, *Crossing Unmarked Snow: Further Views on the Writer's Vocation* and *The Way It Is: New and Selected Poems*. Stafford's memoir, *Down in My Heart: Peace Witness in War Time*, first published in 1947, was reprinted in 1998 with an introduction by his son, Kim Stafford.

HENRY TAYLOR won the Pulitzer Prize for Poetry in 1986 for his third volume of poems, *The Flying Change*. His most recent book, *Understanding Fiction: Poems, 1986–1996*, was published in 1996. He is also the author of a textbook, *Poetry: Points of Departure* and *Compulsory Figures: Essays on Recent American Poets*. Taylor is a translator of classical drama, including works by Euripides, Plautus, and Sophocles. He worked for many years as a poet-in-the-schools and has been a riding instructor since 1962. Taylor has taught for the last twenty-five years at American University in Washington, D.C.

NANCE VAN WINCKEL is the author of three books of poems, including *The Dirt* and *After a Spell*. She is also the author of two books of short stories, *Limited Lifetime Warranty* and *Quake*. She worked as a poet-in-the-schools in North Idaho in 1973–1974. Van Winckel currently teaches at Eastern Washington University where she began an outreach program for EWU graduate programs in Spokane, Washington, schools and prisons.

DAVID WAGONER is the author of ten novels, including *The Hanging Garden* and *Whole Hog*, and fifteen books of poems, including *Who Shall Be the Sun?* and *In Broken Country*. His most recent book of poems is *Walt Whitman Bathing*. Wagoner edited *Straw for the Fire: From the Notebooks of Theodore Roethke, 1943–1963*. He has been the editor of *Poetry Northwest* since 1966 and has taught at the University of Washington in Seattle since 1954.

RON WALLACE is the author of ten books of poetry and criticism, including *The Uses of Adversity*, *The Makings of Happiness*, and *God Be with the Clown: Humor in American Poetry*. Wallace has worked as a substitute teacher in St. Louis middle schools, and he currently directs the creative writing program at the University of Wisconsin–Madison. He

serves as editor for the University of Wisconsin Press Poetry Series.

BRUCE WEIGL is the author of seven collections of poetry, most recently *What Saves Us* and *Sweet Lorain*. He also has edited three collections of critical essays on American poets. Weigl has translated poems from captured documents from the Vietnamese with Nguyen Thanh. With Kevin Bowen, Weigl coedited the anthology *Between the Lines: Writing from the Joiner Center Workshop*, and with Bowen and Nguyen Ba Chung, he coedited and cotranslated *Mountain River: Vietnamese Poetry from the Wars*. Weigl teaches at Pennsylvania State University, where he directs the M.F.A. in Writing program.

DON WELCH is the author of eight books of poems, most recently *Fire's Tongue in the Candle's End* and *A Brief History of Feathers*. Welch taught for two years in high schools in Colorado and Nebraska, and he has worked for twenty years as a poet-in-residence for the Nebraska Arts Council in kindergarten through twelfth-grade classes, in urban to one-room rural schools.

REED WHITTEMORE is the author of sixteen books of poetry, essays, critical reviews, and biography, including *The Poet as Journalist: Life at the New Republic* and *William Carlos Williams: Poet from Jersey.* His most recent book of poems is *The Past, The Present, The Future: Poems Selected and New,* published in 1990. Whittemore has held several editorial positions, including literary editor of *New Republic* from 1969 to 1973 and editor of *Delos* from 1987 to 1991. He was Consultant in Poetry to the Library of Congress from 1964 to 1965, and he has taught at many colleges and universities, including Princeton University, the University of the South, and the University of Maryland, where he has been professor emeritus since 1984.

DARA WIER's most recent books of poems include *The Book of Knowledge* and *Our Master Plan.* She taught grades seven to twelve for one year at Prince Edward County High in Farmville, Massachusetts. She has also taught poetry writing at every level and is a regular visiting poet to schools in Amherst, Massachusetts. Wier has taught at many universities including the University of Utah, Bowling Green State University, and the University of Texas. She currently teaches at the University of Massachusetts at Amherst.

ROSEMARY WILLEY's first book, *Intended Place,* won the 1996 Stan and Tom Wick Poetry Prize. She has published poems in *Poetry, Crazyhorse, Ploughshares,* and other journals. Willey currently teaches at a senior center in

Kalamazoo, Michigan. She is also a visiting poet at a local Montessori school, where they are launching the Kalamazoo-Pushkin Elementary Poetry Exchange Project in order to exchange student poetry with an elementary school in Pushkin, Russia.

GREG WILLIAMSON won the Nicholas Roerich Poetry Prize in 1995 for his first book, *The Silent Partner.* From 1990 to 1995 he taught elementary and secondary students in an extracurricular school in Baltimore, Maryland, called the Center for Smart Learning. Williamson currently teaches at Johns Hopkins University.

ANDREW WILSON has published poetry in *Descant* and critical articles in *Mississippi Quarterly* and *Hemingway Review.* He was a student teacher of high school English at Maumee High School in Maumee, Ohio, and also taught for two summers in the secondary school program, Upward Bound, at Kent State University in Kent, Ohio. He currently teaches at William Rainey Harper College in Palatine, Illinois.

DAVID WOJAHN's books of poetry include *The Falling Hour, Late Empire, Mystery Train,* and *Ice House Lights,* which won the 1981 Yale Series of Younger Poets Prize. He taught in poets-in-the-schools programs in Arizona (1978 to 1980) and Louisiana

(1981 to 1982). Wojahn currently teaches at Indiana University and is on the field faculty of the Vermont College M.F.A. in Writing program.

JAMES WRIGHT's first book, *The Green Wall*, won the 1957 Yale Series of Younger Poets Prize. His other books of poems include *The Branch Will Not Break, Shall We Gather at the River,* and *This Journey*, which was published posthumously in 1980. In his lifetime Wright translated poems of Pablo Neruda, César Vallejo, Georg Trakl, and Hermann Hesse. His *Collected Poems* won the 1972 Pulitzer Prize in Poetry. *Above the River: The Complete Poems of James Wright* was published in 1990.

AL YOUNG is the author of twenty books, including *Heaven: Poems 1956–1990* and *Conjugal Visits.*

His novels include *Who Is Angelina?, Sitting Pretty,* and *Seduction by Light.* He is also the author of three books about music, *Drowning in the Sea of Love (Musical Memoirs), Kinds of Blue,* and *Bodies & Soul,* which won an American Book Award from the Before Columbus Foundation. Young has taught for thirty years in colleges, schools, and communities.

PAUL ZIMMER is the author of eleven books of poems including *Crossing to Sunlight: Selected Poems, Big Blue Train,* and *The Great Bird of Love,* which was selected by William Stafford as a 1989 National Poetry Series winner. He taught in the Pennsylvania poets-in-the-schools program from 1970 to 1978. For the past thirty years Zimmer has worked in scholarly publishing.

Permissions

We are grateful to the authors who have given us permission to include previously unpublished work in this anthology. We also thank the authors, editors, and publishers who have given us permission to reprint poems.

KATHLEEN AGUERO, "Beating up Billy Murphy in Fifth Grade," from *The Real Weather*, Hanging Loose Press. Copyright © 1987 by Kathleen Aguero. Reprinted by permission of the author.

SHERMAN ALEXIE, "At Navajo Monument Valley Tribal School," from *The Business of Fancy Dancing*, Hanging Loose Press. Copyright © 1992 by Sherman Alexie. Reprinted by permission of Hanging Loose Press.

DICK ALLEN, "Janes Avenue," from *Ode to the Cold War: Poems New and Selected*, Sarabande Books. Copyright © 1997 by Dick Allen. Reprinted by permission of the author.

MAGGIE ANDERSON, "Spitting in the Leaves" and "The Thing You Must Remember," from *Cold Comfort*, University of Pittsburgh Press. Copyright © 1986 by Maggie Anderson. Reprinted by permission of the University of Pittsburgh Press.

RANE ARROYO, "Spanish Lessons," originally in *The Heartlands Today: A Cultural Quilt Issue*, Firelands Writing Center. Copyright © 1992 by Rane Arroyo.

Reprinted by permission of the author.

JAN BEATTY, "Saving the Crippled Boy," from *Mad River*, University of Pittsburgh Press. Copyright © 1995 by Jan Beatty. Reprinted by permission of the University of Pittsburgh Press.

ROBIN BECKER, "A History of Sexual Preference," from *All-American Girl*, University of Pittsburgh Press. Copyright © 1996 by Robin Becker. Reprinted by permission of the University of Pittsburgh Press. "Hockey Season," from *Backtalk*, Alice James Books. Copyright © 1982 by Robin Becker. Reprinted by permission of the author.

ROBERT BLY, "Gratitude to Old Teachers," from *Meditations on the Insatiable Soul*, HarperCollins Publishers. Copyright © 1995 by Robert Bly. Reprinted by permission of the author and HarperCollins Publishers.

RICHARD BRAUTIGAN, "Gee, You're So Beautiful That It's Starting to Rain," from *The Pill Versus the Springhill Mine Disaster*, Houghton Mifflin Company. Copyright

printed by permission of the author.

DONALD HALL, "Spring Glen Grammar School," originally in *The New Yorker* and reprinted in *The Best American Poetry 1992*, ed. Charles Simic, Macmillan Publishing Company. Copyright © 1991 by Donald Hall. Reprinted by permission of *The New Yorker* and the author.

JAMES HARMS, "Busing." Copyright © 1999 by James Harms. Published by permission of the author. "Field Trip to My First Time," from *The Joy Addict*, Carnegie-Mellon University Press. Copyright © 1997 by James Harms. Reprinted by permission of the author.

MARC HARSHMAN, "Lunch." Copyright © 1999 by Marc Harshman. Published by permission of the author.

DAVID HASSLER, "Reaching to a Sky of Soba," from *Whiskey Island Magazine*, Cleveland State University. Copyright © 1998 by David Hassler. Reprinted by permission of the author.

JUDY PAGE HEITZMAN, "The Schoolroom on the Second Floor of the Knitting Mill," originally in *The New Yorker*. Copyright © 1991 by Judy Page Heitzman. Reprinted by permission of *The New Yorker* and the author.

CONRAD HILBERRY, "Instruction." Copyright © 1999 by Conrad Hilberry. Published by permission of the author.

EDWARD HIRSCH, "Execution," from *The Night Parade*, Alfred A. Knopf Inc. Copyright © 1989 by Edward Hirsch. Reprinted by permission of Alfred A. Knopf Inc.

DAVID HUDDLE, "The School," from *The Nature of Yearning*, Gibbs M. Smith, Inc. Copyright © 1992 by David Huddle. Reprinted by permission of the author.

T. R. HUMMER, "The Beating," from *The Passion of the Right-Angled Man*, University of Illinois Press. Copyright © 1984 by T. R. Hummer. Reprinted by permission of the author.

PAUL B. JANECZKO, "Bonfire," from *Brickyard Summer*, Orchard Books. Copyright © 1989 by Paul Janeczko. Reprinted by permission of the author.

ALLISON JOSEPH, "Day-Tripping," from *In Every Seam*, University of Pittsburgh Press. Copyright © 1997 by Allison Joseph. Reprinted by permission of the University of Pittsburgh Press. "Junior High Dance," originally in *Unsettling America: Race and Ethnicity in Contemporary American Poetry*, ed. Jennifer Gillian and Maria Mazziotti Gillian, Viking Penguin, and reprinted in *Soul Train*, Carnegie-Mellon University Press. Copyright © 1994 by Allison Joseph. Reprinted by permission of the author.

JULIA KASDORF, "How My Father Learned English." Copyright © 1998 by Julia Kasdorf. Published by permission of the author. "Catholics," from *Sleeping Preacher*, University of Pittsburgh Press. Copyright © 1992 by Julia Kasdorf. Reprinted by permission of the University of Pittsburgh Press.

BRIGIT PEGEEN KELLY, "The Teacher," from *To the Place of Trumpets*, Yale University Press. Copyright © 1988 by Brigit Pegeen Kelly. Reprinted by permission of the author.

JANE KENYON, "Learning in the First Grade" and "Trouble with Math in a One-Room Country School," from *Otherwise: New & Selected Poems*, Graywolf Press. Copyright © 1996 by the estate of Jane Kenyon. Reprinted by permission of Graywolf Press.

KENNETH KOCH, "Schoolyard in April," from *Poetry* (Chicago). Copyright © 1947 by Kenneth Koch. Reprinted by permission of the author.

FRANK KOOISTRA, "School Buses." Copyright © 1999 by Frank Kooistra. Published by permission of the author.

MAXINE KUMIN, "The Nuns of Childhood: Two Views," from *Looking for Luck*, W. W. Norton and Company, Inc. Copyright © 1992 by Maxine Kumin. Reprinted by permission of W. W. Norton and Company, Inc.

DORIANNE LAUX, "Homecoming," from *What We Carry*, BOA Editions, Ltd. Copyright © 1994 by Dorianne Laux. Reprinted by permission of the author.

LI-YOUNG LEE, "Persimmons,"

from *Rose*, BOA Editions, Ltd. Copyright © 1986 by Li-Young Lee. Reprinted by permission of BOA Editions, Ltd.

PHILIP LEVINE, "Among Children" and "M. Degas Teaches Art & Science at Durfee Intermediate School," from *What Work Is*, Alfred A. Knopf Inc. Copyright © 1991 by Philip Levine. Reprinted by permission of Alfred A. Knopf Inc.

LARRY LEVIS, "Childhood Ideogram," from *Winter Stars*, University of Pittsburgh Press. Copyright © 1985 by Larry Levis. Reprinted by permission of the University of Pittsburgh Press.

JULIA LISELLA, "Raising Their Hands," from *Ark*, New York University. Copyright © 1988 by Julia Lisella. Reprinted by permission of the author.

CHRIS LLEWELLYN, "The Grade School I Attended Was Next to a Slaughterhouse," from *Steam Dummy & Fragments from the Fire*, Bottom Dog Press. Copyright © 1993 by Chris Llewellyn. Reprinted by permission of the author.

AUDRE LORDE, "Brother Alvin," from *Collected Poems*, W. W. Norton and Company, Inc. Copyright © 1978 by Audre Lorde. "Teacher," from *Collected Poems*, W. W. Norton and Company, Inc. Copyright © 1973 by Audre Lorde. Reprinted by permission of W. W. Norton and Company, Inc.